# Lyrics *on* *Several* *Occasions*

# Lyrics

## on Several Occasions

A SELECTION OF STAGE & SCREEN LYRICS
WRITTEN FOR SUNDRY SITUATIONS; AND NOW
ARRANGED IN ARBITRARY CATEGORIES. TO
WHICH HAVE BEEN ADDED MANY INFORMATIVE
ANNOTATIONS & DISQUISITIONS ON THEIR WHY
& WHEREFORE, THEIR WHOM-FOR, THEIR HOW;
AND MATTERS ASSOCIATIVE.

## by Ira Gershwin, *Gent.*

ELM TREE BOOKS
HAMISH HAMILTON · LONDON

First published in Great Britain 1977 by Elm Tree Books/Hamish Hamilton Ltd, 90 Great Russell Street, London WC1B 3PT. Copyright © 1959 by Ira Gershwin. SBN 241 89634 7. Printed and bound in Great Britain by Redwood Burn Limited, Trowbridge and Esher

---

*for L.S.G.*

How these curiosities would be quite forgott, did not such idle fellowes as I am putt them downe!

*John Aubrey:* BRIEF LIVES:
*"The Digbys and Venetia Stanley"*

# FOREWORD

*The Uniqueness.* When I was asked by the publisher to do a book of my lyrics plus some commentary, I wasn't too taken aback since it had been my suggestion that I do one. Having been asked, I went to work—without, however, a contract: this, in case I didn't like what I would turn out and up with. Two years later, not entirely displeased with what, off and on, I was at, I signed. And now, almost two years after that—finally—my first book. And my last, I hope, because the prose it contains I found just as difficult, bemusing, and time-consuming as, originally, its lyrics. And since song lyrics have supported me (and the government) reasonably well, whereas prose wouldn't keep me in cigars—therefore: if nothing else, this book is unique in that its author isn't looking forward to doing another.

*The Purpose.* What has been attempted is a presentation of various examples of stage and screen lyric-writing: rhymed entities which individually, after merging with music, suited some plot situation or background, or the special capabilities of the performers, or a following ensemble dance—or any combination of these and other requirements.

*The Lyrics.* Some of the selections are from songs still, happily, fairly well known. For the most though are included little-known and unknown ones. But practically all are from songs and other musical forms which have been performed on stage or screen; and nearly all have previously seen print in sheet music, in folios, or in published librettos. (The dozen or so appearing for the first time are asterisked in the title index.) Beneath each title I have placed an entry of the lyric's associations—naming first the production involved and its date; then the composer; next, quoted from the printed music, is the style or tempo direction; then follow

vii

the names of the original performers; after these credits, a line or so usually indicates the background or situation.

*The Procedure.* With variety and range to be the keynote, I scanned and screened seven or eight hundred items (from some forty or so entertainments), the words not only of solo songs but of duets, trios, openings, excerpts from musical sequences, &c. Knowing that many of the lyrics would run rather long, I thought that about seventy would be ample. But some peculiar amplification-compulsion took over, and now there are about one hundred. These I sorted, grouping together four or more of somewhat similar sentiment, each conjointment to fit, fittingly or loosely, a category.

*The Categories.* As stated on the title page, the categories are arbitrary. Some are valid: e.g., the lyrics contained in the section called "Divers Duets" are duets. But some headings, succumbing to other alliteration and to paronomasia, aren't that categorical— their holdings frequently pertaining only in a far-fetched way to the classification. An example of this roundabout conformity obtains in the "Sound Effects" category. The title of one lyric, "Applause, Applause," and the word "Laughed" in the title of another ("They All Laughed") pass some sort of muster. Then I included " 'S Wonderful" because the note following the lyric mentions sibilance. Next comes "Let's Call the Whole Thing Off," because the song concerns itself with pronunciation. Then "Do, Do, Do" shows up because it features a "do, do" and "done, done" reduplicative sound effect. That arbitrary.

*The Commentary.* At the back of the book there were to be notes on the genesis of some of the songs. I figured that about ten thousand words should do it. Very early, though, I found that as I assembled more and more lyrics, more and more were the memories; and more and more was the time I was spending checking dates and occasions, looking over hundreds of old worksheets and much filed correspondence, doing research of a sort, and so on. And little by little some of the annotations were becoming longer and longer. Came the day when I felt that the back section might eventually be carrying too back-breaking a load, and that a better arrangement would be to place each note directly after its lyric. Good. Then, somewhat later, parental solicitude: two thirds of the lyrics, those I hadn't considered notes for, were beginning to look like forlorn stepchildren. So I decided to try for something for all, or nearly all. And that's why the notes are now of all sorts: technical, digressive, autobiographical, ruminative, skippable, long, short. . . . And that's why what started out to be a book of lyrics (plus some commentary) seems to have become a book of commentary (plus illustrative lyrics).

In conclusion, all I have to say is that if the reader finds the book a self-indulgent one, I cannot disagree.

I.G.
Beverly Hills, Calif.

**P.S.** Since most of the lyrics in this lodgment were arrived at by fitting words mosaically to music already composed, any resemblance to actual poetry, living or dead, is highly improbable.

# Acknowledgments

*A* *cquiring* permissions to reprint song lyrics takes a bit of doing, as music-publishers are most possessive of their catalogues. So, a bow to Leonard S. Saxe, my legal advisor, who did most of the doing. And many thanks to the publishers involved: Max Dreyfus of Chappell and Co., Herman Starr of Music Publishers Holding Corporation, Edwin H. Morris of Harwin Music Corporation, Harry Warren of Four Jays Music Co., and M. Scopp of Leo Feist, Inc. A bow also to Lawrence D. Stewart, co-author of *The Gershwin Years,* for several good suggestions. And my apologies to any dinner guest who may have felt he was singing for his supper by having to listen to a couple of the notes in progress. As for publishers Blanche and Alfred Knopf—they couldn't have been nicer.

# CONTENTS

# Contents

# Contents

# Contents

# The Not Impossible He

*"The Man I Love"*

*"Looking for a Boy"*

*"My Son-in-Law"*

*"Sure Thing"*

# THE MAN I LOVE

LADY, BE GOOD! (1924). Music, George Gershwin. Verse: *"Andantino semplice"*; refrain, "slow." For Adele Astaire.

When the mellow moon begins to beam,
Ev'ry night I dream a little dream;
And of course Prince Charming is the theme:
    The he
    For me.
Although I realize as well as you
It is seldom that a dream comes true,
    To me it's clear
    That he'll appear.

### Refrain

Some day he'll come along,
  The man I love;
And he'll be big and strong,
  The man I love;
And when he comes my way,
I'll do my best to make him stay.

He'll look at me and smile—
  I'll understand;
And in a little while
  He'll take my hand;
And though it seems absurd,
I know we both won't say a word.

Maybe I shall meet him Sunday,
    Maybe Monday—maybe not;
Still I'm sure to meet him one day—
    Maybe Tuesday
    Will be my good news day.

He'll build a little home
    Just meant for two;
From which I'll never roam—
    Who would? Would you?
And so all else above,
I'm waiting for the man I love.

---

*Much Ado about "The Man I Love"; or, 3 Strikes and Out.* In the spring of 1924 when I finished the lyric to the body of a song—the words and tune of which I now cannot recall—a verse was in order. My brother composed a possibility we both liked, but I never got around to writing it up as a verse. It was a definite and insistent melody—so much so that we soon felt it wasn't light and introductory enough, as it tended to overshadow the refrain and to demand individual attention. So this overweighty strain, not quite in tune as a verse, was, with slight modification, upped in importance to the status of a refrain. I gave it a simple set of words, then it had to acquire its own verse; and "The Man I Love" resulted.

As an originally intended verse it appears, undated, in George's early 1924 notebook between pieces dated April 4 and 24. It consists of the familiar eight-bar theme which repeats itself and is followed by a "vest" (songwriter jargon for the ending of a verse, usually two lines, leading to the refrain or chorus). This vest was somewhat expanded to become the "release"—or "middle" or "bridge"—and then the opening theme was repeated again for the last eight bars. Clear? Confusing? Anyway, that's what was done.

When *Lady, Be Good!* was being prepared, Maecenas Otto H.

4

Kahn was approached as a potential investor. He listened to the set-up, said it sounded like a success; therefore he wasn't interested. He helped financially only those shows, ballets, and other artistic ventures which were worth doing but which must inevitably reach the point of no returns. Then either George or producer Aarons happened to mention that "The Man I Love"—which Kahn had heard some time before at a party—would be in the new show. "Well," reflected Kahn, "that's worth something. All right, put me down for ten thousand." (The following year when he got back not only his money but a dividend greater than his investment, he wrote Aarons and Freedley thanking them for a unique experience—the first time he had ever received any return from a theatrical venture.)

When the show opened in Philadelphia, Adele Astaire, solo, sang the song charmingly and to an appreciative hand. But sweetness and simplicity in style do not make for the vociferous applause given dancing duets and novelty numbers. So, after a week, "The Man I Love" was withdrawn. Actually the show was in good shape and the elimination required no replacement, as the show was a bit long anyway.

In New York somewhat later, Lady Mountbatten asked George for an autographed copy of the published song. (In those days the music-publisher thought nothing of putting out five to seven numbers for the out-of-town theater-lobby sales. Today scarcely any sheet music is sold that way; in its stead a brisk business seems to have arisen in souvenir programs.) On her return to London, Lady Mountbatten had her favorite band, the Berkeley Square Orchestra, make a special arrangement for their concerts. Soon other London bands were playing it more or less correctly by ear, since the published song hadn't been released there. And from London it spread to Paris, where it was played frequently by several Negro combinations. So, some performance and no sales over there, while much less happened over here.

Three years later, Edgar Selwyn, for whom we were doing *Strike Up the Band,* insisted the song be introduced in the score of that otherwise satirical operetta. So in late August 1927, "The Man I Love" again was havened between footlights and backdrops.

5

But this first version of *Strike Up the Band,* after a half-week in Long Branch, New Jersey (there were any number of tryout theaters and towns before the movies talked) and two weeks in Philadelphia, had to close because of lack of business. ("Awful!" said a man sitting behind me in Long Branch. "Father, I think it's just wonderful!" said his daughter.) Once more was this hapless song orphaned.

It was a busy year. Not only had we musicalized *S.U.T.B.* but also *Funny Face.* Sometime in October, while we were day-and-nighting it on the road doing a plastic job on the latter, we finally agreed to join forces as soon as possible with Romberg and Wodehouse on the rush-job score of *Rosalie* for Ziegfeld. Actually we'd been approached about this project before and had blocked out two or three numbers for it, in case.

And again "The Man I Love." Suddenly Ziegfeld wanted it in *Rosalie* for Marilyn Miller. We informed him this would be up to Selwyn, who still wasn't unsold on *S.U.T.B.* and expected to put it on again one day. On October 28, 1927, this telegram: "GEORGE GERSHWIN ROOM 705 SYLVANIA HOTEL PHILADELPHIA PENN—FEEL SENTIMENTAL ABOUT THE MAN I LOVE AS IT WAS RESPONSIBLE FOR DOING MUSICAL SHOW STOP WOULD HATE TO LOSE IT BUT IF YOU FEEL KEENLY ABOUT IT WILL DO ANYTHING TO PLEASE YOU STOP REGARDS EDGAR SELWYN." Ziegfeld must have worked on Selwyn, because we really weren't *that* keen about the number. Personally, by this time I was bored with it as a possible show song. However, Marilyn Miller was Broadway's biggest musical star; fine—maybe she could do something with it.

After *Funny Face* opened successfully, we went immediately on to *Rosalie,* already in rehearsal. It was a hectic period for two librettists, Bolton and McGuire; two composers, Romberg and Gershwin; and two lyricists, Wodehouse and myself. But somehow this show—based on mythical-kingdom royalty visiting the U.S., in turn based on the recent visit of Marie, Queen of Rumania—managed to make its scheduled Boston opening on time—and even became a big hit.

"The Man I Love"? Keeping the title, I rewrote most of it—twice, I think—to fit possible plot cues for Miss Miller. And? Well,

6

it certainly wasn't in the show opening night. For that matter, there were so many switches in the score that I can't recall Miss Miller ever even rehearsing it.

But Max Dreyfus, our publisher, still had faith in it and felt it oughtn't remain so comatose. He told us that if we cut our sheet-music royalty a cent each (production sheet music generally paid six cents: three cents each for music and lyric) some money could be afforded for exploitation. We cut, he exploited, and the song began to be heard quite a bit and sold fairly well—within six months about one hundred thousand copies, plus several good recordings.

That, however, wasn't the end. The thrice-orphaned song was adopted by Helen Morgan and sister singers who kept on vocalizing whatever virtues it had; and it has since led a fairly active and respectable life for over thirty years, thanks also to dozens of recordings and uses in motion pictures.

*Mildly Ironic Addendum.* In December 1929, *Strike Up the Band,* after a major job of rewriting by Morrie Ryskind and ourselves, was produced by Edgar Selwyn to critical acclaim. But the song he loved wasn't in it. Its popularity by this time precluded any possible use in the score—and a probable fourth ousting.

# LOOKING FOR A BOY

TIP-TOES (1925). Music, George Gershwin. *"Moderato."*
Queenie Smith as "Tip-Toes" Kaye in "one"—i.e., downstage
while the set was being changed behind the drop.

If it's true that love affairs
Are all arranged in Heaven,
My Guardian Angel's holding out on me.
So, I'm looking for a boy
'Bout five foot six or seven,
And won't be happy till I'm on his knee.
I'll be blue until he comes my way;
Hope he takes the cue when I am saying:

*Refrain*

I am just a little girl
Who's looking for a little boy
Who's looking for a girl to love.

Tell me, please, where can he be,
The loving he who'll bring to me
The harmony I'm dreaming of?

It'll be good-bye, I know,
To my tale of woe
When he says, "Hello!"

So,

I am just a little girl
Who's looking for a little boy
Who's looking for a girl to love.

---

I notice that in her yearned-for's requirements the vocalist mentions merely desired height: " 'bout five foot six or seven." Matters

not background, earning capacity, taste in breakfast foods, or even the color of his eyes. Obviously a damsel easily pleased. But about the only rhymes I could use for "Heaven" were "seven" and "eleven"; hence her preoccupation with height. ("Devon" was geographically out-of-bounds; Laborite E. Bevin was probably already married; and what could one do with "replevin"?)

Luckily, talented Queenie Smith was tiny, and Allen Kearns, who played opposite her, was only a couple of mites taller.

*       *       *

I thought I knew most of the terms for the classification of rhyme: masculine, feminine, double, triple, near, eye, assonantal, internal, &c. But Babette Deutsch's recent and scholarly *Poetry Handbook* reveals half a dozen I'm sure I'd never come across before. One term especially intrigues me: "Apocopated rhyme, so called because the end of one rhyming word is cut off." Examples given are: "say" to rhyme with the first syllable of "crazy"; "Spain" with the first of "gainless."

Why titillated at this late stage? Because I am suddenly made aware that long, long ago in the last two verse lines of "Looking for a Boy" the music made me rhyme, apocopatedly, "way" with "saying"; and I now feel one with Molière's M. Jourdain the day he learned he'd been speaking prose for over forty years.

*       *       *

"*Moderato,*" as musical style direction, seems to have been the term most favored on sheet music in the early Twenties. There were many exceptions, of course, and gradually more specific and imaginative terms in Italian or English began to be introduced. Notably different in the Twenties were the terms used by Spencer Williams for his "Banjo Blues," "Rock Pile Blues," and other of his compositions. Williams combined the Italian and American in "Tempo di weary," "Tempo disappointo," "Tempo di Sadness," and other highly individual directions.

The most precise—and whimsical—instructions, though, were

9

by modernist Erik Satie, who, a generation earlier, insisted his music be played "dry as a cuckoo, light as an egg" or "like a nightingale with a toothache," and such. And when it comes to the provocative or singular titles dubbed on many LP albums these days, it could be that such titles of Satie's as "Airs to Make You Run Away" or "Flabby Preludes for a Dog" were precursors.

# MY SON-IN-LAW

PARK AVENUE (1946). Music, Arthur Schwartz. "Dreamily."
Mrs. Sybil Bennett and one of her early husbands, Mr. Richard
Nelson, are co-parents of a daughter engaged to a young man who
is not in Dun and Bradstreet. This is not their idea of a son-in-law.
Sung by Leonora Corbett and Raymond Walburn.

*Sybil*

Ever since my little girl was a little girl
I've dreamed of the man of her dreams—
    Not merely one who'd love her,
    But also be worthy of her:
The sort of Prince Charming the world esteems.
    Let me draw
My picture of the perfect son-in-law.

*Refrain*

    He will be six foot two,
        My son-in-law;
    His haircut will be crew,
        My son-in-law.
At Princeton he was crowned the hero of the gridiron;
He once beat Bobby Jones and only used a midiron.
    He'll take me out to dance,
        My daughter's groom;
    Our rumba will entrance
        The Persian Room.
I'll be the envy of all women who'll find him divine,
For—nothing's too good for a daughter of mine.

*Nelson*

    Some day he'll come along,
        My son-in-law;
    His strongbox will be strong,
        My son-in-law.

11

His oil and lumber lands so great they can't be mapped in;
So loaded he need never tip a night club captain.
    I'll travel on his yacht—
       Belay, below!
    For music he'll be hot—
       And back a show;
And I'll be meeting all the lovelies in the chorus line,
For—nothing's too good for a daughter of mine.

*Sybil (apostrophizing)*

    So, join our entourage,
      Dear son-in-law;
    She's meant for your menage,
      Dear son-in-law.
The one she yearns for now is really an absurd one;
But bide your time—you'll be the second or the third one.
    She's bound to come around—
      You'll have your nest.
    Meanwhile, keep on compound-
      Ing interest.
The style of living she's accustomed to I'll not resign,
    With minks and chinchillas
    And mansions and villas . . .
    And how she rejoices
    In yachts and Rolls-Royces,
    And portraits by Dali,
    Green orchids from Bali;
    Then, parting divinely,
    You treat her benignly
    With trust funds bewild'rin'
    And the custody of the children.
You'll do the proper thing—no sacrifices you'll decline,
For—nothing's too good for a daughter of mine,

---

The musical trick in the last line to emphasize the lyrical twist was brought about by an acceleration of tempo for the phrase "nothing's too good for a daughter of mine." (Frequently, on the other hand, special emphasis can be obtained by a deceleration, as, say, in slowing up the last line, "Won't you tell me how?" of "Nice Work If You Can Get It" to "Won't—You—Tell—Me—How?")

It will be noticed that the third refrain—the one in which Sybil apostrophizes—is longer than the others. This ten-line amplification of wistful wishing is an example of extension which occasionally can be done to build up the exit refrain; actually it is a sort of incorporated patter. But of course there is no rule about this device: you either feel it or don't.

# SURE THING

COVER GIRL (1944). Music, Jerome Kern. "Moderately."
A pre-World War I music-hall number with a race-track background and backdrop. Sung by Rita Hayworth and Ensemble.

The favorite doesn't always win,
    No matter what the odds.
Since nobody knows how they'll come in—
    I leave it to the gods.
        So wish me luck—
Because I'm going to bet on
    A sentimental hunch
I'm somehow suddenly set on.

### Burthen

Somehow I'm sure I've found a sure thing
        In you.
        Something within
        Tells me we'll win.
Somewhere my heart has picked you out of
        The blue;
And since I'm only a beginner,
        A winner
        I'll be.
But, win or lose, whatever comes up,
        You're thumbs up
        With me.
One thing I'm sure I'm sure of
        All my life through:
If love can figure out a sure thing,
        That sure thing is you.

---

*Forgotten Melody.* In 1939 when Kern was between assignments, I wrote nine or ten songs with him. Nothing ever happened to them, although both of us liked several. During this period he played me many other tunes I liked but just didn't get around to. Some four years later, *Cover Girl* period, I tried to remind him of a lovely tune of the earlier period by humming a snatch of it. But he had never put it on paper, and couldn't recall it. I told him his daughter Betty had been very fond of this melody, so he called her in and between us and our snatches, it came back to him. "Good tune," he said. "What about it?" I told him it had begun haunting me that morning, and if he could split the opening note into two notes, I had a two-word on-the-nose title for the flashback number in the film—one which had a production idea for the choreographer and the designer. When he heard the title, "Sure Thing," with its race-track background, he said: "Of course— nothing to it—in fact, the two notes make a better announcement."

In working on the song, however, it turned out that the on-the-nose title could be more advantageously placed within the first line, rather than at the start of it; and the double notes made place for the words "somehow" and "somewhere."

$$*\qquad*\qquad*$$

After finishing the verse and refrain we added a patter in waltz tempo. This is how it began:

*Men*

After the races are over,
  After the races are run—
    Loser or winner,
    Let's go out to dinner—
  And let's have a little,
  Let's have a little fun.

Let's go to Rector's or Shanley's.
  Champagne and duck are in line.
    Let's lose our troubles
    Imbibing those bubbles—
  Oh, let's have a little,
  Let's have a little wine.

15

Then followed the suggestion that after dinner what about a drive along Riverside Drive? But the lady wasn't having any:

> *Maribelle*
> No drive in the country for me after dark;
> My limit is just once around Central Park.

(In those days Central Park after dark was quite safe and unmuggable.)

$$* \quad * \quad *$$

*Burthen.* Since the days of the Greeks, the word "Chorus" has had, and still has, many usages. Its special use as the heading for the body of a song (following the introductory portion, or "Verse") goes back about a hundred and fifty years and is still the prevalent one in popular song. "Refrain," some centuries old, was the term for a phrase recurring at intervals, especially at the end of stanzas —but around the turn of this century it began to be substituted for "Chorus" in the publication of musical-comedy and operetta songs. "Burthen," a variant of "Burden," was the term Kern always preferred to "Refrain" or "Chorus" in his published output. (I notice, though, that in the memorial *The Jerome Kern Song Book* his editors have seen fit to drop "Burthen" for the more usual "Refrain.")

# Divers Duets

*"Aren't You Kind of Glad We Did?"*

*"The Babbitt and the Bromide"*

*"Could You Use Me?"*

*"Embraceable You"*

*"The Half of It, Dearie, Blues"*

*"I Don't Think I'll Fall in Love Today"*

*"If I Became the President"*

*"That Certain Feeling"*

# AREN'T YOU KIND OF GLAD
# WE DID?

THE SHOCKING MISS PILGRIM (1946). Music (posthumous), George Gershwin. "Moderato—in conversational style." On an afternoon off, Cynthia Pilgrim of New York (Betty Grable), Boston's first typist (1874), is shown the city's sights by her employer, John Pritchard (Dick Haymes). Subsequently they take supper at a most respectable restaurant. Then, as he is seeing her home in a cab, both suddenly realize the enormity of their social crime: no chaperone. Momentarily, though, they aren't bothered.

### John

Oh, it really wasn't my intention
To disregard convention;
It was just an impulse that had to be obeyed.

### Cynthia

Beacon Hill behavior we've been scorning,
But I'll not go in mourning—
Though my reputation is blemished, I'm afraid.

### John

What's done, is done.
But wasn't—and isn't—it fun?

### Refrain

Honestly, I thought you wouldn't;
Naturally, you thought you couldn't.
And probably we shouldn't—
    But aren't you kind of glad we did?
Actually, it all was blameless;
Nevertheless, they'll call it shameless.
So the lady shall be nameless,
    But, aren't you kind of glad we did?

19

### Cynthia

Socially, I'll be an outcast:
Obviously we dined alone.
On my good name there will be doubt cast—
With never a sign of any chaperone.

### John

No matter how they may construe it—
Whether or not we have to rue it—
Whatever made us do it—
    Say, aren't you kind of glad we did?

### Second Refrain

### Cynthia

Honestly, I thought I wouldn't;
Naturally, I thought I couldn't.
And probably I shouldn't—

### John

    But, aren't you kind of glad we did?
The community will call me viper.

### Cynthia (*agreeing*)

The opportunity should have been riper.

### Both (*harmonizing*)

We'll have to pay the piper—
    But, what we did we're glad we did.

### Cynthia

Supper was quite above suspicion;
Milk in the glasses when they'd clink.

### John (*nodding*)

Listening to a tired musician—

## Divers Duets

*Cynthia*

But what is it Mrs. Grundy's going to think?

*John* (*grace notes added*)

I'm a rounder, a bounder, a cad, a Boston blighter—

*Cynthia* (*also more syllabic*)

You shouldn't be seen alone with your typewriter.

*Both*

Let's turn to something brighter:
  Whatever we did, we're glad we did.

---

This song was written in the early Thirties with no particular show in mind, but intended for the following spot if ever it came up: a young couple in love takes a chance and gets married, despite the fact that they are practically penniless. The words of the refrain began exactly as is, but the release and last section were:

  Socially, I'm rather hazy;
  Financially, I've not a dime.
  Realistically, we're both ka-ra-zy—
    But we'll have one hell of a time.
  Though creditors may try to floor us,
  Though relatives will carp and bore us—
  For us no anvil chorus!
    Whatever we did we're glad we did.

Since no libretto ever called for the situation, this nuptial notion gathered dust for a dozen years. But I liked the tune; and, for *The Shocking Miss Pilgrim,* was able to rework the lyric, changing it from an Epithalamium of the Depression to a Mid-Victorian Colloquy.

\*        \*        \*

21

The innocent and innocuous "Aren't You Kind of Glad We Did?" was filmed most charmingly. I realized, though, that without visual viewing the song would be considered improper by those who didn't listen too well. So, for the printed sheet music I changed the "vest" from:

> What's done, is done.
> But wasn't—and isn't—it fun?

to:

> With just one kiss,
> What heaven, what rapture, what bliss!

thus making all morally impeccable. To no avail, however. A few recordings were pressed, but the song was banned from the air by the networks.

\*      \*      \*

For "(posthumous)" cf. note to "The Back Bay Polka."

# THE BABBITT AND THE BROMIDE

FUNNY FACE (1927). Music, George Gershwin. *"Allegretto humoroso."* Specialty number sung and danced by Fred and Adele Astaire.

### 1

A Babbitt met a Bromide on the avenue one day.
They held a conversation in their own peculiar way.
They both were solid citizens—they both had been around.
And as they spoke you clearly saw their feet were on the
  ground:

### Refrain

> Hello! How are you?
> Howza folks? What's new?
> I'm great! That's good!
> Ha! Ha! Knock wood!
> Well! Well! What say?
> Howya been? Nice day!
> How's tricks? What's new?
> That's fine! How are you?

Nice weather we are having but it gives me such a pain:
I've taken my umbrella, so of course it doesn't rain.

> Heigh ho! That's life!
> What's new? Howza wife?
> Gotta run! Oh, my!
> Ta! Ta! Olive oil! Good bye!

### 2

Ten years went quickly by for both these sub-sti-an-tial men,
Then history records one day they chanced to meet again.
That they had both developed in ten years there was no doubt,
And so of course they had an awful lot to talk about:

23

*Refrain*

Hello! How are you? &c.
I'm sure I know your face, but I just can't recall your name;
Well, how've you been, old boy, you're looking just about the
    same.
Heigh ho! That's life! &c.

3

Before they met again some twenty years they had to wait.
This time it happened up above, inside St. Peter's gate.
A harp each one was carrying and both were wearing wings,
And this is what they sang as they kept strumming on the
    strings:

*Refrain*

Hello! How are you? &c.
You've grown a little stouter since I saw you last, I think.
Come up and see me sometime and we'll have a little drink.
Heigh ho! That's life! &c.

---

"It needs work" unquestionably applied to *Funny Face* when it
opened in Philadelphia and looked like a failure. We were on the
road six weeks, and everyone concerned with the show worked day
and night, recasting, rewriting, rehearsing, recriminating—of re-
joicing, there was none. "The Babbitt and the Bromide" was the
final change. It went in on a Thursday or Friday night in Wilmington, when the audience consisted of no more than two hundred—
mostly pretty and young and pregnant Du Pont matrons (my wife's
observation). The number was introduced at 10:50 and concluded
with Fred and Adele doing their famous "run-around"—to show-
stopping applause—and suddenly, with all the other changes, the
show looked possible. The week's business in Wilmington totaled
$6,000. The following week we opened the new Alvin Theatre in
New York and grossed $44,000.

\*     \*     \*

## Divers Duets

Although our conception for performance of "Babbitt-Bromide" was that all the lines be sung in unison by Fred and Adele (as a dead-pan conversation carried on with neither listening to the other), they immediately felt it would be more effective nonsense to offer the phrases by turns:

> Fred: Hello!
> Adele: How are you?
> Fred: Howza folks?
> Adele: What's new? &c.

Which presentation too was fine with us. Therefore the placement of this lyric in a duet category.

\*  \*  \*

Fred and Vinton (Vinton Freedley, co-producer) won't recall this, but I made a mental note at the time: The day my brother and I demonstrated the song, Fred took me aside and said: "I know what a Babbitt is, but what's a Bromide?" Just about an hour later, in the Wilmington Hotel elevator, Vinton said to me: "I was brought up on Gelett Burgess and the Goops, so I know what a Bromide is—but what's a Babbitt?"

# COULD YOU USE ME?

GIRL CRAZY (1930). Music, George Gershwin. *"Moderato."*
Sung by Allen Kearns as Danny Churchill, Eastern playboy, and
Ginger Rogers as Molly Gray, Western cowgirl and postmistress.

*Danny*

Have some pity on an Easterner;
   Show a little sympathy.
No one possibly could *be* sterner
   Than you have been with me.
There's a job that I'm applying for—
   Let me put it to you thus:
It's a partnership I'm dying for—
   Mr. and Mrs. Us!
Before you file it on the shelf,
Let me tell you of myself.

*Refrain*

Oh, I'm the chappie
To make you happy:
I'll tie your shoes-ies
And chase your blues-ies;
   Oh, lady, would you—
   Oh, tell me, could you
     Use me?

If we've no butler,
I'll put the cutler-
Y on the table
As well's I'm able;
   I'd slave as few could,
   If only you could
     Use me.

26

## Divers Duets

Do you realize what a good man
    You're getting in me?
I'm no Elk or Mason or Woodman
    Who gets home at three.

    The girls who see me
    Grow soft and dreamy,
    But I'm a gander
    Who won't philander.
        Oh, could you use me?
'Cause I certainly could use you!

### Molly

There's a chap I know in Mexico
    Who's as strong as he can be;
Eating nails and drinking Texaco—
    He is the type for me.
There is one in California,
    More romantic far than you. . . .
When he sings "Ha-Cha-Cha-Chornia,"
    I often think he'll do.
But as for you, sir, I'm afraid
You will never make the grade.

### Refrain

    For you're no cowboy;
    You're soft—and how!—boy!
I feel no muscle
That's fit for tussle.
        I must refuse you;
        I cannot use you.
           'Scuse me!

No night life for you,
The birds would bore you,
The cows won't know you,
A horse would throw you—
        You silly man, you,
        To ask me, "Can you
           Use me?"

Though at love you may be a wizard,
  I'm wanting to know:
Could you warm me up in a blizzard,
  Say, forty below?

  Your ties are freakish;
  Your knees are weakish;
  Go back to flappers
  And high-ball lappers!
    Though you can use me,
I most certainly can't use you!

---

Just as in films, where scenes are seldom shot in sequence, so with work in progress on a musical: songs are rarely written in the order the audience later hears them. That is, a song for a situation in the second act may be the first number completed, while an opening for the show may be—and usually is—the last. The attraction-repulsion duet "Could You Use Me?" was written for an early meeting between characters Danny and Molly. Several scenes later, now on a far friendlier basis, they sang "Embraceable You," a song which happened to have been written two years before "Could You Use Me?" (Cf. note to "Embraceable.")

P.S. Molly couldn't remain that stand-offish in "Could You Use Me?" for an entire evening. Somewhere late in the second act, with wedding bells in the welkin offing, this was a reprise:

  I'll make a mother
  Like no one other,
  If you could bother
  To be the father.
    Oh, could you use me,
'Cause I certainly could use you!"

# EMBRACEABLE YOU

GIRL CRAZY (1930). Music, George Gershwin. Verse: "Whimsically"; refrain: "Rhythmically." Eastern playboy Danny Churchill finally overcomes the prejudices of Custerville (Ariz.)'s young postmistress, Molly Gray. Sung by Allen Kearns and Ginger Rogers.

### Danny

Dozens of girls would storm up;
 I had to lock my door.
Somehow I couldn't warm up
 To one before.
What was it that controlled me?
 What kept my love-life lean?
My intuition told me
 You'd come on the scene.
Lady, listen to the rhythm of my heart beat,
 And you'll get just what I mean.

### Refrain

Embrace me,
My sweet embraceable you.
 Embrace me,
 You irreplaceable you.
Just one look at you—my heart grew tipsy in me;
You and you alone bring out the gypsy in me.
 I love all
The many charms about you;
 Above all
I want my arms about you.
Don't be a naughty baby,
Come to papa—come to papa—do!
My sweet embraceable you.

*Molly*

I went about reciting,
   "Here's one who'll never fall!"
But I'm afraid the writing
   Is on the wall.
My nose I used to turn up
   When you'd besiege my heart;
Now I completely burn up
   When you're slow to start.
I'm afraid you'll have to take the consequences;
   You upset the apple cart.

*Refrain*

   Embrace me,
My sweet embraceable you.
   Embrace me,
You irreplaceable you.
In your arms I find love so delectable, dear,
I'm afraid it isn't quite respectable, dear.
   But hang it—
Come on, let's glorify love!
   Ding dang it!
You'll shout "Encore!" if I love.
Don't be a naughty papa,
Come to baby—come to baby—do!
My sweet embraceable you.

---

In the summer of 1928 my brother and I were busy on an operetta version of *East Is West* for Ziegfeld. We were most enthusiastic about this project, which was to star Marilyn Miller and Clark and McCullough. Approximately one half of the score had been completed when, alas, Mr. Ziegfeld read J. P. McEvoy's snappy *Show Girl* (whose heroine was Dixie Dugan, a Ziegfeld Girl). In his hypnotically persuasive manner (always great charm until a contract was signed) Ziegfeld managed to have us postpone

the operetta and start on *Show Girl*. *Show Girl* wasn't much—
it cost much and lost much—and, unfortunately, *East Is West,*
whose production would have cost much more, never happened.
Most of the *East Is West* music had Oriental overtones, but there
were several musical-comedy numbers: "Embraceable You" was
one, and we found a spot for it in *Girl Crazy*. Among other salvable
music were "Lady of the Moon," which was later lyricized to
"Blah, Blah, Blah" for the film *Delicious;* and "In the Mandarin's
Orchid Garden," which was published as a concert song.

\*     \*     \*

"Embraceable" is rather unusual as a more or less sentimental
ballad in that some of its rhymes are four-syllable ones: "embraceable you—irreplaceable you," and (in a reprise) "silk and
laceable you"; "tipsy in me—gypsy in me." Also, there is a trick
four-syllable one in: "glorify love—'Encore!' if I love."

\*     \*     \*

Incidentally, the song was one of my father's favorites. Whenever
possible, with company present, his request to George was: "Play
that song about me." And when the line "Come to papa—come
to papa—do!" was sung, he would thump his chest, look around the
room, and beam.

# THE HALF OF IT, DEARIE, BLUES

LADY, BE GOOD! (1924). Music, George Gershwin. "Smoothly."
Fred Astaire as Dick Trevor; Kathlene Martyn as Shirley Vernon.

### 1. (*Dick*)

Each time you trill a song with Bill
Or look at Will, I get a chill—
    I'm gloomy.
I won't recall the names of all
The men who fall—it's all appall-
    Ing to me.
Of course, I really cannot blame them a bit,
For you're a hit wherever you flit.
    I know it's so, but dearie, oh!
    You'll never know the blues that go
      Right through me.

### Refrain (A)

I've got the You-Don't-Know-the-Half-of-It-Dearie Blues.
The trouble is you have so many from whom to choose.
    If you should marry
    Tom, Dick, or Harry,
    Life would be the bunk—
    I'd become a monk.
I've got the You-Don't-Know-the-Half-of-It-Dearie Blues!

### Refrain (B)

I've got the You-Don't-Know-the-Half-of-It-Dearie Blues.
Will I walk up the aisle or only watch from the pews?
    With your permission
    My one ambition
    Is to go through life
    Saying, "Meet the wife."
I've got the You-Don't-Know-the-Half-of-It-Dearie Blues!

# Divers Duets

## 2. (*Shirley*)

You dare assert that you were hurt
Each time I'd flirt with Bill or Bert—
    You brute, you!
Well, I'm repaid: I felt betrayed
When any maid whom you surveyed
    Would suit you.
Compared to you, I've been as good as could be;
Yet here you are—lecturing me!
    You're just a guy who makes me cry;
    Yet though I try to "cut" you, I
       Salute you.

### Refrain

I've got the You-Don't-Know-the-Half-of-It-Dearie Blues.
Oh, how I wish you'd drop an anchor and end your
    cruise.
       You're just a duffer
       Who makes me suffer;
       All the younger set
       Says your heart's to-let.
I've got the You-Don't-Know-the-Half-of-It-Dearie Blues!

---

*The Blues.* As a term for depressed spirits, "the blues" goes back to the first decade of the nineteenth century: "and I saw he was still under the influence of a whole legion of the blues" (Washington Irving: *Salmagundi,* 1807). Irving's phrase was his shortened version of the earlier British and Scottish "the blue devils," which figuratively meant a visitation by the spirits of Melancholia. A century went by before The Blues began to be used as a music term; this, thanks principally to the talent and output of W. C. Handy and his world-famous "St. Louis Blues," "The Memphis Blues," and many more.

Generally—not necessarily always—an Afro-American Blues is a melancholy-mooded musical entity of homesickness or love double-crossed or economic grievance, intoned on stanzas of three lines, using four bars to a line; and is a solo song. Spirituals, the more sacred voicings, are essentially group songs. And unquestionably both The Blues and Spirituals have greatly enriched American music.

Some sort of grievance is featured in the musical-comedy adaptation of The Blues as evidenced here in "The Half of It, Dearie, Blues" and in the Kern-Caldwell "Left All Alone Again Blues"—but of course in such as these the lyric approach isn't attempting to plumb the melancholy depths of the real Blues.

34

# I DON'T THINK I'LL FALL
# IN LOVE TODAY

TREASURE GIRL (1928). Music, George Gershwin. *"Moderato."* Gertrude Lawrence, Ann; Paul Frawley, Neil: two who care but are cautious.

### 1

Ann: Just think of what love leads to:
   Maybe to marriage—maybe divorce.
Neil: Into a jam love speeds two;
   It may be Nature's course,
    But we mustn't be
    Like the other sheep.
Ann:   Better far if we
    Look before we leap.
Both: Perhaps it's better after all
   If we don't answer Nature's call.

#### Refrain

Neil:   Who knows if we'd agree?
    You like you and I like me.
  I don't think I'll fall in love today.
Ann:   When evening shadows creep,
    I like dancing—
Neil:       I like sleep.
  I don't think I'll fall in love today.
Ann:   Still it might be fun to bring
     Your carpet slippers;
    When the dinner bell would ring,
     I'd serve a can of kippers.
Neil:   Don't you know how to cook?
Ann:   I could look in a book.
Neil: I don't think I'll fall in love today.

2

Neil: Love is a fever chronic;
    We can avoid it—why take a chance?
Ann: Safer to be platonic;
    Why burn up with romance?
Neil:     Adam without Eve
    Happiness had known,
    So suppose we leave
    Well enough alone.
Ann: Imagine signing up for life,
    Then finding peas roll off his knife.

*Refrain*

Neil:     D'you sleep with window shut?
Ann:     Window shut.
Neil:                Charming, but—
    I don't think I'll fall in love today.
Ann:     Did you pick that cravat?
Neil:     I did that.
Ann:                Here's your hat.
    I don't think I'll fall in love today.
Both:     It's as clear as A B C
    We're not agreeing;
    Incompatibility
    The judge would be decreeing.
    When all is said and done,
    Seems we two will never be one.
    Let's, oh, let's not fall in love today!

---

*Title Adaptation.* I doubt that the title of this duet would have come to me if at some time or other I hadn't read Chesterton's "A Ballade of Suicide" with its refrain of "I think I will not hang myself today." (Not that the other lines and content of the ballade and those of the duet have anything in common.) And since I'm telling what this title was adapted from, nothing can prevent me at this point from telling, in a highly skippable paragraph, about another adaptation: the title of this book.

One day while rearranging some books in section P, I was placing Matthew Prior's *Poems on Several Occasions* to the left of *Puniana* (London, 1867) when I suddenly thought what an appropriate title *Lyrics on Several Occasions* could be, *my* occasions of course being stage and screen. Quite excited at first, my enthusiasm began to wane after a bit: too literary perhaps; also I had visions of Prior turning over in his Westminster Abbey grave. No, it wouldn't be right; I'd better get something else. Then two nights later I was reading an article in a *Colophon* and saw a reference to *Poems upon Several Occasions* by Mrs. Aphra Behn. Interesting. About a week later I was looking up poet and songwriter Henry Carey—I forget why—and he too had published a *Poems on Several Occasions*. Really interesting now. So I got hold of a *Cambridge Bibliography* and discovered that there was a period a couple of centuries back when at least a dozen others had published *Poems on, &c.* Which finding freed me for *Lyrics on, &c.*, with no further apprehension about a possible revolving Prior.

*     *     *

*Treasure Girl's* plot was concerned with a treasure hunt which took the proceedings to the Caribbean and, after a couple of months, took us all to Cain's Warehouse. There was some excellent dialogue by Vincent Lawrence and—if I may—the songs and dances, thanks to a brilliant cast headed by Miss Lawrence and Clifton Webb, were well—even rapturously—received. But, some songwriters to the contrary, numbers alone do not make a show.

# IF I BECAME THE PRESIDENT

STRIKE UP THE BAND (1930). Music, George Gershwin. *"Allegro Moderato."* Washington hostess Mrs. Draper propositions the Unofficial Spokesman, Colonel Holmes. Played by Blanche Ring and Bobby Clark.

*Mrs. D.:*  If I made you the ruler
Of this great democracy—
*Col. H.:*  Then I'd make you First Lady,
Which is reciprocity.
*Mrs. D.:*  Imagine how delightful life
Will be when we're on top.
*Col. H.:*  Just think! No matter where we'd go
They'd make the traffic stop.
*Both:*  We'd beat King Solomon in all his glory.
Oh, ev'rything would be just hunky-dory.

### *Refrain*

*Col. H.:*  If I became the President,
*Mrs. D.:*  And I were the President's wife,
*Both:*  We'd shake the hand of ev'ryone we'd see.
*Col. H.:*  We could receive ambassadors,
*Mrs. D.:*  The kind the upper class adores,
*Both:*  And have the whole Supreme Court down for tea.
*Col. H.:*  I'll talk on trade conditions.
*Mrs. D.:*  We'll open expositions,
*Both:*  And proudly march behind the drum and fife.
*Mrs. D.:*  Oh, it thrills me just to tell of it!
*Col. H.:*  We both would be on vel-a-vit—
If I became the President,
*Mrs. D.:*  And I were the President's wife.

38

# Divers Duets

## Second Refrain

*Col. H.:*    If I became the President,
*Mrs. D.:*    And I were the President's wife,
            You'd flood the Senate with your orat'ry.
*Col. H.:*    I'd make each politish-i-on
            Prohibit Prohibish-i-on—
*Both:*    A hundred million drinkers would be free.
*Col. H.:*    I'd grow a beard, I'm thinkin'.
*Mrs. D.:*    You'd be as great as Lincoln,
            And Mister Hearst would surely print your life.
*Col. H.:*    But I'd never go so far afield
            As Tyler, Polk or Gar-a-field—
            If I became the President,
*Mrs. D.:*    And I were the President's wife.

---

The references to Prohibition and to newspaper mogul W. R. Hearst make this, from today's viewpoint, a period piece. I do like, though, going not so far afield as Tyler, Polk or Gar-a-field. But there was more than appears above.

One day in the Boston tryout Bobby Clark, unfortunately for me, came up with four penciled pages of new lyrics (which I still have) he himself had written for possible encores. I shuddered when I saw them. No actor had ventured to change or add to my lyrics before this; besides, these were pretty terrible, with rhymes like "cellar—vanilla" (some weren't bad: "decorum—floor um"). Since Bobby was one of the great comedians in an era when three or four top ones ruled the musical-comedy roost, management asked me to go along with him as far as possible. I was able to make some corrections and to cut the encores down to two; but unable to do anything with some lines he insisted on. My favorite couplet of his:

> And just to show we're home-like
> We'll bathe in the Potomac.

P.S. Imperfect rhymes or not, I am unhappy to report that his lines received as many chuckles as did mine.

# THAT CERTAIN FEELING

TIP-TOES (1925). Music, George Gershwin. *"Moderato Semplice."* Steve (Allen Kearns) and Tip-Toes (Queenie Smith) in an at once sentimental and rhythmic duet.

### Steve

That certain feeling—
The first time I met you.
I hit the ceiling,
I could not forget you.
You were completely sweet;
Oh, what could I do?
I wanted phrases
To sing your praises.

That certain feeling—
The one that they all love—
No use concealing
I've got what they call love.
Now we're together
Let's find out whether
You're feeling that feeling too.

### Tip-Toes

That certain feeling—
The first time I met you.
That certain feeling
I could not forget you.
I felt it happen
Just as you came in view.
Grew sort of dizzy;
Thought, "Gee, who *is* he?"

## Divers Duets

That certain feeling—
I'm here to confess, it
Is so appealing
No words can express it.
I cannot hide it,
I must confide it:
I'm feeling that feeling too.

---

There are some vocal recordings of this song wherein the singer misses the rhythmic point of the tune by giving equal value to the first three notes and words of such lines as:

The first time I met you.
I could not forget you.
I've got what they call love, &c.

which should be heard as:

(Beat) *Thefirst* time I met you
(Beat) *Icould* not forget you
(Beat) *I'vegot* what they call love, &c.

\*     \*     \*

*That Certain Question: "Which Comes First?"* When I was on jury service in New York many years ago there was a case found for the defendant. Afterwards, in the corridor, I saw the lawyer for the plaintiff approaching and thought I was going to be lectured. But no. Greetings over, all he wanted to know was whether the words or the music came first.

Every songwriter has been put this question many times, and by now nearly all interested know that no rule obtains: sometimes it's the lyric and sometimes the tune. And sometimes—more often than not these days—the words and music are written practically at the same time: this, when collaborators are at work together (in the same room, that is—though I have heard of collaboration on

41

the telephone); and a song, sparked either by a possible title or by a likely snatch of tune, emerges line by line and section by section. (*What* comes first, according to show-writers in demand, is the contract.)

With the great art-song writers of the Elizabethan Age (John Dowland, Thomas Campion, half a dozen others), the words always came first, even though many of these highly talented men were also fine composers and wrote their own lute accompaniments. But already in that period were numerous instances where lyrics were fitted to music. This was done by satirists and parodists who, discarding the words of folk song and ballad, penned—quilled, if you like—new lyrics to the traditional tunes—lyrics which politicized, thumbed the nose, eulogized, or went in for out-and-out bawdry. (Lyric-transformation played quite a part also in early hymnody. In Germany, for instance, Martin Luther was a notable example of the hymnist who took many a secular song, well known to the people, and, retaining the tune, threw out the worldly lyric to substitute one of spiritual quality.)

The practice of putting new words to pre-existent song became more and more common and led to the beginnings of ballad opera. England's outstanding opus in this realm was Gay's *The Beggar's Opera,* London, 1728. This was so successful that it ran sixty-two nights, a new theatrical record that "stood unchallenged for almost a century." In the Heinemann edition (London, 1921) I count sixty-eight short "airs"—chosen by Gay from the great store of English, Irish, and Scottish melodies—newly lyricized by the playwright.

Everyone knows that in the Gilbert-and-Sullivan operettas practically all the lyrics were written first. However, earlier in Gilbert's theatrical career he'd also had plenty of experience setting words to music. In the 1860's many extravaganzas and burlesques of his, based on Continental operas, were produced in London. These were adapted by him into English with tricky lyrics and recitatives loaded with puns. Among them were Meyerbeer's *Robert le Diable,* which became *Robert the Devil; or The Nun, the Dun, and the Son of a Gun,* and Bellini's *Norma,* extravagandized to *The*

## Divers Duets

*Pretty Druidess; or The Mother, the Maid and the Mistletoe Bough.*

\* \* \*

My favorite account of how songs are written was told me second-hand many years ago. At a Christmas party in a music-publishing house a shipping-clerk was explaining to an impressed friend how hit-writer Walter Donaldson (who had just written both the words and the music of a hit) went about it: "Well, you see—he sort of gets the scope of the thing and then scopes it out."

# The Possessive Case

*"They Can't Take That Away from Me"*

*"My Ship"*

*"He Hasn't a Thing Except Me"*

*"Who Cares?"*

*"Mine"*

*"My One and Only Highland Fling"*

# THEY CAN'T TAKE THAT AWAY
# FROM ME

SHALL WE DANCE (1937). Music, George Gershwin. "Lightly, and with feeling." Fred Astaire to Ginger Rogers on the ferry to Hoboken.

> Our romance won't end on a sorrowful note,
> > Though by tomorrow you're gone;
> The song is ended, but as the songwriter wrote,
> > "The melody lingers on."
> They may take you from me,
> > I'll miss your fond caress.
> But though they take you from me,
> > I'll still possess:

### Refrain

> The way you wear your hat,
> > The way you sip your tea,
> The mem'ry of all that—
> No, no! They can't take that away from me!

> The way your smile just beams,
> > The way you sing off key,
> The way you haunt my dreams—
> No, no! They can't take that away from me!

> We may never, never meet again
> > On the bumpy road to love,
> Still I'll always, always keep
> > The mem'ry of—

The way you hold your knife,
    The way we danced till three,
    The way you've changed my life—
No, no! They can't take that away from me!
No! They can't take that away from me!

---

Studying this lyric, I see that the release could have been improved to:

We may never, never meet again
    On the bumpy road to love,
Still I don't know when
    I won't be thinking of—
The way you hold your knife . . .

which would rhyme "again" and "when" on important notes where no rhyme now exists; also, the sequence "I don't know when I won't" contains a double negative, a form of phrasing I sometimes find myself favoring over a simple affirmative.

Half an hour later. If the above had occurred to me originally, I'd have kept it. But now after some reflection—no dice. Despite the rhyme and the indirect affirmative, "always, always" following "never, never," plus all the "No, no!"s make a better-balanced refrain. So, *stet!*

\*　　　\*　　　\*

"They Can't Take That Away from Me" was a Best Song nominee in the Academy of Motion Picture Arts and Sciences "Oscar" awards. And since then, if I check correctly, only two others of mine have been nominated: "Long Ago and Far Away" and "The Man That Got Away." These three songs have two things in common: (1) in the final voting none won; and (2) the title of each contains the word "away." So? So—away with "away"?

48

# MY SHIP

**LADY IN THE DARK** (1941). Music, Kurt Weill. *"Andante espressivo."* Sung by Gertrude Lawrence. Supposedly a turn-of-the-century song known to Liza Elliott in her childhood.

> My ship has sails that are made of silk,
>> The decks are trimmed with gold;
>>> And of jam and spice
>>> There's a paradise
>>> In the hold.
>
> My ship's aglow with a million pearls,
>> And rubies fill each bin;
>>> The sun sits high
>>> In a sapphire sky
>> When my ship comes in.
>
>>> I can wait the years
>>> Till it appears—
>>> One fine day one spring.
>>> But the pearls and such,
>>> They won't mean much
>>> If there's missing just one thing:
>
>> I do not care if that day arrives—
>>> That dream need never be—
>>>> If the ship I sing
>>>> Doesn't also bring
>>> My own true love to me—
>>> My own true love to me.

---

*Missing Song.* "My Ship" loomed significantly in the unconscious of successful—but unhappy—magazine editor Liza Elliott. It was important to the analysis that Liza recall completely this song and what happened in her childhood when last she sang it. Although the lyric itself was a mental block to her until well into the second act, the haunting tune—orchestrated by Kurt to sound sweet and simple at times, mysterious and menacing at other—heightened the suspense of many moments in the play.

Later, when *Lady in the Dark* was filmed, the script necessarily had many references to the song. But for some unfathomable reason the song itself—as essential to this musical drama as a stolen necklace or a missing will to a melodrama—was omitted. Although the film was successful financially, audiences evidently were puzzled or felt thwarted or something, because items began to appear in movie-news columns mentioning that the song frequently referred to in *Lady in the Dark* was "My Ship." I hold a brief for Hollywood, having been more or less a movie-goer since I was nine; but there are times. . . .

\* \* \*

During the writing of a song, it is sung repeatedly, word by word and line by line, by lyricist and/or composer, be their voices fetching, raucous, or even nonexistent. This is done to keep testing the singability and clarity in sense and sound. Careful as one tries to be, however, occasionally an aural ambiguity is overlooked. For two weeks of rehearsals, Miss Lawrence sang "My Ship" with its original release:

> I can wait for years
> Till it appears,
> One fine day one spring.

Then, one afternoon session, she sang these lines as she had done previously, stopped, fixed me with a look (I was in the fourth or fifth row), and demanded: "Why *four* years, why not five or six?" She was quite right, and I quickly told her to change *"for* years" to *"the* years." Somehow neither Kurt nor I had noticed that preposition "for" received the same musical value as "wait" and "years."

50

# HE HASN'T A THING EXCEPT ME

ZIEGFELD FOLLIES OF 1936. Music, Vernon Duke. Leaning against a lamppost and looking forlorn, the one and only Fanny Brice is discovered. The lamppost walks off and Fanny begins:

Let me introduce a gentleman
High class people call a louse;
Not a very sentimental man—
Nothing you'd want 'round the house.
    Oh, I really can't tell
    Why I'm under his spell;
The chances are slim
I'll ever see what I see in him.

*Refrain*

I give you his highness,
A pain worse than sinus.
Though I felt all hopped up
The minute he popped up,
    It's easy to see
He hasn't a thing except me.

I help out his brother,
Pay rent for his mother;
Feel when I took him in
I carry his women.
    He's living for free,
And hasn't a thing except me.

He's *Mon Homme;*
He can take my heart and break it—
Mend it when he starts to clown.
    Just a bum—
But the guy can make me take it
When he ups and lets me down.

51

Though I brought this on me,
How long can he con me?
Still, it's not too late for
The day that I wait for:
   The day he'll agree
He hasn't a thing except me.

(*At end of number, lamppost walks on to join Fanny in a bow.*)

---

In the middle of the second refrain, the lyric stopped to have Fanny say:

Well, you get the idea. You know, I've been singing about this bum for twenty-five years under different titles and making a pretty good living out of him. He's always the same lowlife, always doing me dirt, but I keep on loving him just the same. Can you imagine if I really ever met a guy like that what I would do to him?

At this point, the conductor would rap impatiently, and Fanny get back into character.

Most of the couplets in the second refrain would be, from today's view, period ones—e.g.:

His talk isn't flow'ry,
It's straight from the Bow'ry. . . .
Oh, he is the soul with
Whom I'd share the dole with. . . .
The one thing he's mastered
Is just getting plastered. . . .
Of money he's got less
Than someone who's potless. . . .

In this age when terms of aberration are generally better known than they were a generation ago, I probably would have had her reflect in her wonderful Bronxese:

## The Possessive Case

He's maybe sadistic?
And me, masochistic?

*     *     *

Fanny was one of the most versatile and accomplished personalities in our musical theater. In this particular *Follies,* for example, she put over this torch song, and did a wonderful burlesque of modern dancing, following her singing of "Modernistic Moe." In the skits she played Baby Snooks; then a tough Tenth Avenue girl; then the most elegant English drawing-room matron in "Fawncy, Fawncy"; then a Bronx housewife who has misplaced her winning Sweepstakes ticket; then a starlet in a satire on Hollywood musicals —all exquisitely and incomparably executed.

# WHO CARES?

OF THEE I SING (1931). Music, George Gershwin. "Brightly."
The White House newsmen ask President Wintergreen what he
intends doing about Miss Devereaux, the girl he has jilted. William
Gaxton and Lois Moran.

*Wintergreen*

It's a pleasant day.
That's all I can say.

*Reporters*

People want to know
What of Devereaux? . . .

*Wintergreen*

Here's some information
I will gladly give the nation:
I am for the true love—
Here's the only girl I do love. . . .

*Mrs. Wintergreen*

I love him and he loves me
And that's how it will always be—
So what care we
    About Miss Devereaux?

*Both*

Who cares what the public chatters?
Love's the only thing that matters.

# The Possessive Case

*Refrain (to each other)*

Who cares
If the sky cares to fall in the sea?
Who cares what banks fail in Yonkers
Long as you've got a kiss that conquers?
Why should I care?
Life is one long jubilee
So long as I care for you—
And you care for me.

---

*A Change of Mood.* In any musical show, sometimes the same musical sequence can be repeated with lyrics changed either completely (for, say, new locales as in "Florence" and "Paris") or partially (in second refrains or in finales for new or added sentiments). "Who Cares?," however, is an example of a refrain where, without a rewritten lyric, a musical offering sometimes can be reprised for a change of mood.

Styled "Brightly," this song was sung in that manner—even glibly—by President Wintergreen and the First Lady in their successful attempt to put the reporters off from further heckling about the girl Wintergreen jilted. In a later scene, when impeachment was threatened if he didn't divorce his wife to marry the jiltee, Wintergreen turned down the advice of his Cabinet and embraced his wife. The lights dimmed down, the music slowed up, and the tongue-in-cheek refrain was now sung with such sincerity that this moment became a quite sentimental, even a touching, one.

55

# MINE

LET 'EM EAT CAKE (1933). Music, George Gershwin. Verse: *"Recitativo";* refrain: "Slowly, with much expression"; patter: "Gracefully, lightly." John P. Wintergreen, defeated for a second Presidential term, has organized the Blue Shirts, a movement to overthrow the government. After an inflammatory speech he is cheered by his followers. William Gaxton, Lois Moran, and Ensemble.

### Wintergreen

My good friends, don't praise *me!*
I owe it all to the little woman,
*This* little woman, *my* little woman.
She's the reason for my success.
Why, when I think how we suffered together—
Worried together, struggled together,
Stood together together,
I grow so sentimental I'm afraid
I've got to burst into song.

### Ensemble

Please do!
We'd love to know how you feel about her
And how she feels about you.

### Refrain (*Wintergreen*)

Mine, love is mine,
Whether it rain or storm or shine.
Mine, you are mine,
Never another valentine.
And I am yours,
Tell me that I'm yours;
Show me that smile my heart adores.
Mine, more than divine,
To know that love like yours is mine!

## The Possessive Case

### Patter

(*Ensemble comes downstage and sings the counter-melody directly to audience*)

> The point they're making in the song
> Is that they more than get along;
> And he is not ashamed to say
> She made him what he is today.
> It does a person good to see
> Such happy domesticity;
> The way they're making love you'd swear
> They're not a married pair.
> He says, no matter what occurs,
> Whatever he may have is hers;
> The point that *she* is making is—
> Whatever *she* may have is *his*.

(*Ensemble repeats patter as simultaneously the Wintergreens repeat their refrain. Then Omnes:*)

> Mine, more than divine,
> To know that love like yours is mine!

---

With only fifty-four notes to this stately refrain, and with a one-syllable title, "Mine," fitted in four times, the lyricist couldn't exactly be brilliant in setting the remaining fifty syllables. (I was lucky to get the phrase "never another valentine" to make up for the obvious "more than divine" line.) However, by the supplementing of the refrain with a lyricized counter-melody, then the prefacing of both with a verse more or less *recitativo*, the resultant complete "Mine" made interesting listening.

The use of counter-melody of course goes far back through the musical ages. We ourselves had used it several times before. In *Of Thee I Sing,* for instance, at one point protagonist Wintergreen sings "Some Girls Can Bake a Pie" while two groups, each to a different melodic line, concur with words and rhythms other than

57

his—all the words, of course, lost in the vocal mixture, but three melodies do tickle the ear simultaneously.

The counter-melody of "Mine" was different. When the boys and girls came down to the footlights to point up the absolute togetherness of the Wintergreens, the happily married pair sang their refrain softly, and—most unusual for this sort of thing—the counter-lyric could be understood.

# MY ONE AND ONLY HIGHLAND FLING

THE BARKLEYS OF BROADWAY (1949). Music, Harry Warren. *"Rubato;* very Scotch." Entertainingly burred by Fred Astaire and Ginger Rogers in kilts and tams.

### *Jock*

Though we're called a people of serious mind,
    'Tis often we dance and 'tis often we sing;
And bein' as human as all humankind,
    We aren't superior to havin' a fling.
    I'm takin' the fling of a lifetime,
    The fling of a husband-and-wifetime.

### *Refrain*

    When I went romancin'
I gied no thought to any weddin' ring;
Ev'ry bonny lassie was my highland fling.
    No chance was I chancin';
I'm not the mon you dangle on a string.
I was canny, waitin' for the real, real thing.
        Though I danced each girl
        In the twist and twirl
    Nae one would do.
        An' I went my way
        Till the fatal day
    In the fling I was flung with you.
    Oh, now my heart is prancin',
Drunk as a lord and happy as a king.
        The years I'll weather
        In the hame or on the heather
With my one and only highland fling.

*Patter*

I thought you were fallin' for Andy McPherson.

*Jeannie*

Nae, nae, he became an impossible person.
But what about you and that Connie Mac-
Kenzie?

*Jock*

She talked when I putted and drove me to
frenzy.
But what of the lad known as Bobbie Mac-
Dougal?

*Jeannie*

It pays to be thrifty, but he was too frugal.
An' weren't you daft about Maggie McDermott?

*Jock*

I tasted her cookin'—'twould make me a
hermit.
How jealous I was of MacDonald McCutcheon!

*Jeannie*

His neck had a head on, but there wasn't
much in.

*Jock*

And what about Sandy?

*Jeannie*

His hands were too handy.
And wasn't there Jenny?

*Jock*

I'm nae wantin' any—
I'm nae wantin' any but you.

60

# The Possessive Case

## Jeannie's Refrain

When I went a-dancin'
No special lad I was encouragin';
Ev'ry likely laddie was my highland fling.
No glance was I glancin';
Well, nothin' really worth the mentionin'—
Hopin', watchin', waitin' for the real, real thing.
Though they spoke me soft
In the moonlicht oft,
Nae one would do—
Till it came to pass
To this lucky lass
In the fling I was flung with you.
Oh, now my heart is prancin';
Nothin' about you I'd be alterin'.
The years I'll weather
In the hame or on the heather
With my one and only highland fling.

---

During the first conference on *The Barkleys,* producer Arthur Freed thought a Scottish number for Astaire might be interesting. Neither Harry Warren nor I knew much about Scottish dialect; but, like the girl in the Harbach lyric, we didn't say yes, we didn't say no. After the conference, on our way to inspect the work-cottage the studio had assigned us, I thought of the title with its play on the word "fling." We spent only half an hour in the cottage —it was merely a perfunctory visit because both Warren and I preferred working at home. But while we were there Harry made several tentative attempts at a main theme, one of which we felt good about; and this was the start of the song.

Perhaps the compromise dialect I finally wound up with wouldn't be approved by the student of Scottish lore, but it served its entertainment purpose. For the Scottish surnames in the patter I went through all the Mac's and Mc's in *Who's Who;* also those in the L.A. telephone book. Careful to avoid rhyming "McTavish" and "lavish" because this pairing belonged to Ogden Nash, I went for "MacDougal" and "frugal."

\*     \*     \*

When one does a stage show the published songs have to be ready before the opening, and the authors are usually in New York and can proofread them. But in Hollywood, when one finishes a score it then takes many months before the picture is filmed; and the song proofs and the writers are seldom in touch with one another. To my dismay, when the first published copies of this song reached me in California I found that someone in the New York publishing house had undialected the lyric. A letter of complaint brought an answer from the studio's music-publisher that no sheet-music buyer (if any) would understand the original.

So, another letter of protest. Excerpt:

When practically every English-speaking child in the world sings "Where early fa's the dew" and "Gie'd me her promise true" in "Annie Laurie" I cannot see—even for commercial reasons—why our song had to be emasculated, and "Na' one would do" became "Not one would do" and "hame" became "home" &c. How in the world idiomatic Brooklynese like "spoke real soft" got into the song where "spoke me soft" was indicated is something I'll never understand.

This brought results. A new edition, with the lyric as is, followed.

# With Place Names

*"A Foggy Day (in London Town)"*

*"The Back Bay Polka (Boston)"*

*"Florence (It.)" and "Paris (Fr.)"*

*"Island in the West Indies"*

*"Sweet Nevada"*

*"There's a Boat Dat's Leavin' Soon for New York"*

# A FOGGY DAY
# (IN LONDON TOWN)

A DAMSEL IN DISTRESS (1937). Music, George Gershwin.
Verse: "Rather freely"; refrain: "Brighter but warmly." Sung by
Fred Astaire as Jerry Halliday, an American in London.

> I was a stranger in the city.
>> Out of town were the people I knew.
> I had that feeling of self-pity:
>> What to do? What to do? What to do?
>> The outlook was decidedly blue.
> But as I walked through the foggy streets alone,
> It turned out to be the luckiest day I've known.

### Refrain

> A foggy day in London Town
> Had me low and had me down.
> I viewed the morning with alarm.
> The British Museum had lost its charm.
> How long, I wondered, could this thing last?
> But the age of miracles hadn't passed,
> For, suddenly, I saw you there—
> And through foggy London Town
> The sun was shining ev'rywhere.

---

*From an Album Jacket:* "Early in 1937 . . . Beverly Hills . . .
*A Damsel in Distress.* We had finished three or four songs. One
night I was in the living room, reading. About 1 a.m. George re-

turned from a party . . . took off his dinner jacket, sat down at the piano. . . . 'How about some work? Got any ideas?' 'Well, there's one spot we might do something about a fog . . . how about *a foggy day in London* or maybe *foggy day in London Town?*' 'Sounds good. . . . I like it better with *town*' and he was off immediately on the melody. We finished the refrain, words and music, in less than an hour. ('Do, Do, Do' is the only other . . . in so short a time.) Next day the song still sounded good so we started on a verse."

\*     \*     \*

*Re Next Day and the Verse:* All I had to say was: "George, how about an Irish verse?" and he sensed instantly the degree of wistful loneliness I meant. Generally, whatever mood I thought was required, he, through his instinct and inventiveness, could bring my hazy musical vision into focus. Needless to say, this sort of affinity between composer and lyricist comes only after long association between the two.

\*     \*     \*

There was a different kind of musical communication between George and his earliest Broadway producer. Alex Aarons was quite musical himself and had faith enough to sign George at nineteen for *La, La, Lucille.* Alex was fond at the time of at least twenty of George's tunes which had not yet been written up lyrically, so he had no means of calling for any one of them by numeral or title. But he could request what he wanted to hear this way: Whisking his hand across George's shoulder, he would say: "Play me the one that goes like *that.*" Or: "Play the tune that smells like an onion." Or: *"You* know, the one that reminds me of the Staten Island ferry." And so on. Though this mutual musical understanding didn't develop between them at their first meeting, it didn't take too long. I met Alex a few weeks after George did and in Aarons's apartment heard five or six requests in this oblique manner.

66

Later when George had many tunes on tap for me and I couldn't recall exactly the start of a particular one I wanted to discuss, I would visualize the vocal line and my forefinger would draw an approximation of its curves in the air. And more often than not he would know the tune I meant.

\*     \*     \*

P.S. (months later): I have since been told that this requesting of a tune through the senses of touch or smell or sight may be a form of what the psychologists call *synesthesia:* "a process in which one type of stimulus produces a secondary subjective sensation, as when a specific color evokes a specific smell sensation." (Whether it applies or doesn't, *synesthesia* makes an interesting addition to my vocabulary. I doubt, though, that I'll ever have use for it again.)

# THE BACK BAY POLKA

## (Boston)

THE SHOCKING MISS PILGRIM (1946). Music (posthumous), George Gershwin. "With humorous emphasis." A boardinghouse —Boston, 1874—run by an empathic landlady. A quartet of roomers—a painter, a female lexicographer, a composer, and a poet—calling themselves The Outcasts, carol their sentiments about the city.

### 1

Give up the fond embrace,
Pass up that pretty face;
You're of the human race—
   But not in Boston.

Think as your neighbors think,
Make lemonade your drink;
You'll be the Missing Link—
If you don't wear spats in Boston.

Books that are out of key
   We quickly bury;
You will find liberty
   In Mr. Webster's dictionary.

New York or Philadelph'
Won't put you on the shelf
If you would be yourself—
But you can't be yourself in Boston.

### 2

Don't speak the naked truth—
What's naked is uncouth;
It may go in Duluth—
   But not in Boston.

## With Place Names

Keep up the cultured pose
By looking down your nose;
Keep up the status quos—
Or they'll keep you out of Boston.

At natural history
    We are colossal;
That is because, you see,
    At first hand we study the fossil.

Strangers are all dismissed—
(Not that we're prejudiced)
You simply don't exist—
If you haven't been born in Boston.

### 3

Somewhere the fairer sex
Has curves that are convex,
And girls don't all wear "specs"—
    But not in Boston.

One day it's much too hot,
Then cold as you-know-what;
In all the world there's not
Weather anywhere like Boston.

You're of the bourgeoisie,
    And no one bothers—
Not if your fam'ly tree
    Doesn't date from the Pilgrim
        Fathers.

Therefore, when all is said,
Life is so limit-ed,
You find, unless you're dead,
You never get ahead in Boston.
    You never get ahead,
    Unless you're dead—
You never get ahead in Boston.

*Posthumous Score.* When producer William Perlberg wanted me for *The Shocking Miss Pilgrim* he mentioned two composers, either of whom I'd have been happy to work with. But, approached, each had already contracted for another project. Asked if I had any suggestions, I told Bill that my brother had left much unused musical material; and if the studio would take a chance, I was pretty sure a satisfactory score could be evolved. Perlberg was more than favorably inclined and sold the studio on the idea. So, contracts were drawn up for the Gershwin Estate and for me.

Being no musician, I needed the services of one, and called on Kay Swift. Kay, a composer-musician in her own right, a close friend of George's and mine, was ideal for the job. She knew almost everything George had ever written, had frequently taken down sketches as he composed in his New York apartment, and had total musical recall. (At one time she could play from memory the entire *Porgy and Bess* vocal score of 559 pages.)

We spent ten weeks going carefully through all my brother's notebooks and manuscripts; from them she played and then copied for me well over a hundred possibilities—forty or fifty complete tunes (several of which, such as "Aren't You Kind of Glad We Did?," I had started setting lyrics to in George's lifetime), plus verses, plus themes for arias, openings, &c. During this time I worked also on the lyrics and continued on them for approximately ten more weeks after Kay's work was done. I wound up with a score which pleased Perlberg, screenwriter-director George Seaton, and—just as important to me—me, with: "For You, For Me, For Evermore," a ballad; "One, Two, Three," a waltz; a suffragette number; a Temperance Society theme song, "Demon Rum"; "The Back Bay Polka"; "Changing My Tune"; "Aren't You Kind of Glad We Did?"; and three or four incidental pieces, including a musical montage, "Tour of the Town," which sang the landmarks and historic buildings of then Boston (the 1870's). The music, outside of a few grace notes which I had to add for extra syllables, was all my brother's. So, thanks to Perlberg's trust in the notebooks, manuscripts, and me, a score materialized—the first posthumous one, I believe, for a film musical.

# FLORENCE (IT.)

THE FIREBRAND OF FLORENCE (1945). Music, Kurt Weill.
Excerpt from the musical prologue. Spring 1535. A public square
is filled with public-spirited Florentines come to view the imminent
hanging of B. Cellini.

*Officials*

With nothing but pity the folk we dismiss
Who live in a city that's other than this.

*One Group*

If you're bent on viewing something doing,
　　Come to Florence!
Where is life more active and attractive
　　Than in Florence?
Where are people singing at a swinging—
　　But in Florence?

*All*

Everything warrants
Our singing of Florence—
So, Florence, we're singing of you.

*Another Group*

There's artistic treasure none can measure
　　Here in Florence:
Great is ev'ry statue glowing at you
　　Here in Florence;
And—we've gotta lotta terra-cotta
　　Here in Florence.

*All*

Praises in torrents
We shower on Florence;
Oh, Florence, you always come through!

### Girls

In all of Italy—no brighter star;
We're sitting prettily—right where we are.

### Men

Don't mention Napoli, Venice or Rome;
Sing out (and happily): No place like home!

### Third Group

If you're spending ducats by the buckets—
    You're in Florence.
All the girls are busty. (Love is lusty
    Here in Florence.)
And—did you know that Dante and chianti
    Came from Florence?

### All

    Naught but abhorrence
    For cities not Florence;
Her equal this earth never knew.
    Everything warrants
    Our singing of Florence—
So, Florence, we're singing of you.

# PARIS (FR.)

Naturally, Cellini couldn't hang in the prologue of *The Firebrand* of *Florence,* or we'd have had no show—not that we had. Anyway, toward the end of Act II, he is hired by France's Francis I, and— to the same music and rhythms as "Florence"—now Francophiles take over:

### Officials

With nothing but pity the folk we dismiss
Who live in a city that's other than this.

### One Group

If you're bent on viewing something doing,
　　　Come to Paris!
Music, art and passion set the fashion
　　　Here in Paris.
Have you naught but loathing for your clothing?
　　　Come to Paris.

### All

　　　Paris, oh Paris,
　　　Your riches embarrass!
So, Paris, we're singing of you.

### Another Group

Bottles full of bubbles for your troubles
　　　Pop in Paris.
Paradise is when you read a menu
　　　Here in Paris.
(There's no overlooking what is cooking
　　　Here in Paris.)

### All

　　　Liver with truffle
　　　Makes gourmets unruffle;
Oh, Paris, you always come through!

73

### Girls

Cities in Italy, Sweden or Spain,
(Quite non-committally) give us a pain.

### Men

Don't mention Tripoli, London or Rome;
Sing out hip-hippily: No place like home!

### Third Group

Where have men more talent for what's gallant
    Than in Paris?
Where do girls wear bodices like goddesses—
    But Paris?
(Bodices delightful all are quite full
    Here in Paris.)

### All

Paris, oh Paris—
    Where nothing can harass—
Your equal this earth never knew.
Paris, oh Paris,
    Your riches embarrass!
So, Paris, we're singing of you.

---

*Two Ensemble Numbers, Same Music.* The Prologue to *The Firebrand of Florence* included Song of the Hangman: "One Man's Death Is Another Man's Living"; Civic Song: "Come to Florence"; Cellini's Farewell Song: "Life, Love, and Laughter"; vendors' sales cries; plus recitatives carrying the story line.

Since Chamber of Commerce propaganda wasn't limited to Florentines extolling that city's virtues, we decided to use the music and rhythms of "Florence" late in the second act for similar civic pride by Parisians. Which is why both numbers have the same form in print, although most of the lines are different.

Reprising a song, usually a ballad (sometimes with lines changed to suit the later situation), is standard procedure. (I recall that in 1920's *Mary* the big song hit, "Love Nest," was sung at least six times during the evening by Jack McGowan, not counting a couple of other renditions, one as a duet, the other by the entire company. And who is to say that this was too much of a good thing when the song sold over a million copies?) Technically, however, I wouldn't call "Paris" a reprise of "Florence," even though the same music was listened to in both. I would say the intention was to effect a sort of counterbalance, especially as the longish entities were not in customary song form.

# ISLAND IN THE WEST INDIES

ZIEGFELD FOLLIES OF 1936. Music, Vernon Duke. *"Tempo di Rhumba*—not fast."* Sung by Gertrude Niesen; danced by Josephine Baker and Ensemble.

Let's both of us pack up,
　Sail far from it all;
Tired having to back up
　To the wall.
I know of a place where
　Life really is fun—
Where days are golden
And you're beholden
　To none.
Let's take passage and run!

*Refrain*

Oh, there's an island down in the West Indies
　Ten dollars can buy;
Away from Reuben's and from Lindy's—
　'Neath a tropic,
　Kaleidoscopical sky.

We'll lie around all day and just be lazy—
　The world far behind;
(If that's not heaven then I'm crazy)
　With no taxes
　And with no axes to grind.

　No traffic jams
Under the palm trees by the sea;
　With breadfruit and yams
We'll never need the A & P.

## With Place Names

In that romantic isle in the West Indies—
    No airplanes above—
We'll watch the turtles at their shindies,
    You an' me an'
    The Caribbean
    And love.

### Second Ending

We'll watch the turtles at their shindies;
    Learn the lingos
    Of pink flamingos,
    Where nothing's immoral
    'Way out on the coral,
    Just you an' me an'
    The Caribbean
    And love.

---

*Like I Say.* Since so many writers and speakers these days like "like" as a conjunction, it looks like "like" is being kicked upstairs not only to share the job with "as," but eventually to take over. And, like I say, if that's O.K. with the professors, O.K. by me. And if some used-car salesmen on TV got there because they pronounced "vehicle" "ve-*HICK*-l," I don't take that too serious too.

But if the many who believe that "Car-ib-*BE*-an" should be pronounced "Ca-*RIB*-be-an" become many more, drastic measures will have to be undertaken against the distorters by the composer and me. Why? Because "me an'" and "Ca-*RIB*-be-an" don't rhyme. So, to all "Ca-*RIB*-be-an" lovers: please lay off and give "Car-ib-*BE*-an" and "Island in the West Indies" a chance, as the song is just beginning to get a play. If you must "Ca-*RIB*," at least hold out until 1992, when the song goes public domain.

# SWEET NEVADA

PARK AVENUE (1946). Music, Arthur Schwartz. *"Tempo di Valse Viennoise."* Sung by Leonora Corbett as the much-married Mrs. Sybil Bennett.

## 1

When lady fair
Is deep in despair
And needs a new elixir—
One magical place can fix 'er.
Young woman, go West,
Unfeather your nest!
By car, by train,
Or—better—by plane,
One rushes to arrive there.
Your girlish glands revive there.
Oh, how one feels alive there!

### Refrain

A bill of divorcement
At one time, of course, meant
A lady was dragged in the dust—
Till Nevada saved the day;
Sweet Nevada led the way.

The judge (there's no jury)
Is not from Missouri—
A lady is taken on trust.
In Nevada, hearts are free;
Sweet Nevada—for me!

## With Place Names

### 2

Some states have laws
Quite wretched, because
To claim, let's say, insanity
Might hurt your husband's vanity.
　　Oh, so many grounds
　　Are way out of bounds.
　　Your days you spend,
　　Embarrassed no end
To prove he took a shot at you
Or—panting and looking hot at
　　you—
Much too frequently got at you.

### Refrain

I give you Montana,
Vermont, Indiana—
They still aren't wired for sound.
　　Sweet Nevada, tried and true—
　　My Nevada, I love you.

Although you may seek well,
The like and the equal
On this earth can never be found.
　　Hail Nevada—Arcadee!
　　Sweet Nevada—for me!

### Interlude

Morning sun is singing, "Wake
　　up!
What a lovely day to break
　　up!"
There in Las Vegas
No husbands to plague us—
You go out on horseback
And come with divorce back.

79

3

I'm on my way
Where, yippe aye ay!
They glorify the credo:
Be true to your libido—
　　Where freedom can glow
　　In six weeks or so.
　　One's in the groove
　　Not having to prove
By statutory doses
He's heading for cirrhosis,
You're heading for psychosis.

*Refrain*

I give you my quota
Of Maine and Dakota,
Wisconsin and Michigan, too.
　　Oh Nevada, I am thine.
　　Sweet Nevada, thou art mine.

What spot transatlantic
Is half so romantic?
Who cares if the Danube is blue?
　　Keep Granada! Keep Paree!
　　Save Nevada—for me!

---

Arthur Schwartz and I thought we would be different and do a song about Nevada in an ultra-Viennesy style. And through three weeks of rehearsal our leading lady gave us the elegance we hoped for. But the constant strain on a voice unused to the demands of musical comedy proved too taxing, and opening night in New Haven she could barely project vocally beyond the first few rows. By the time the show reached Philadelphia the song had been completely rewritten. It was no longer a solo but a number with several participants plus a satirical courtroom ballet; and the undulating

## With Place Names

Blue Danube-ish three-quarter-time rip-roared to a clop-clop, plunk-plunk, bang-bang rowdy-dow. "Sweet Nevada's" migration to a more natural musical habitat was happily welcomed by the audience; unhappily, though, after nine weeks in New York, there were no longer any audiences.

Here are excerpts from the verse and refrain, Western Style:

> If marriage you have tackled
> And want to be unshackled . . .
> When on the great decision you've decided—
> Just cross the Great Divide and get divided!

### Refrain

> Out there, out there in Sweet Nevada!
> From top to toe you tingle:
> In six weeks you'll be single. . . .
> They've got a way that's painless
> To make you ball-and-chainless. . . .
> When love is in its gloaming,
> I won't be in Wyoming.
> In Maine and Pennsylvania
> The judges are aloof:
> They seem to have a mania
> For nonsense known as proof.
> Yippee-aye, yippee-O,
> There's just one place to go—
> There's no state like Nevada for me!

# THERE'S A BOAT DAT'S LEAVIN'
# SOON FOR NEW YORK

PORGY AND BESS (1935). Music, George Gershwin. *"Tempo di Blues."* Act III, scene ii: John W. Bubbles as Sporting Life, to Anne Brown as Bess. Catfish Row, Charleston, S.C.

There's a boat dat's leavin' soon for New York.
Come wid me, dat's where we belong, sister.
You an' me kin live dat high life in New York.
Come wid me, dere you can't go wrong, sister.

I'll buy you de swellest mansion
Up on upper Fifth Avenue,
An' through Harlem we'll go struttin',
We'll go a-struttin',
An' dere'll be nuttin'
Too good for you.
I'll dress you in silks and satins
In de latest Paris styles.
All de blues you'll be forgettin',
You'll be forgettin',
There'll be no frettin'—
Jes' nothin' but smiles.

Come along wid me, dat's de place,
Don't be a fool, come along, come along.
There's a boat dat's leavin' soon for New York,
Come wid me, dat's where we belong, sister.
Dat's where we belong!

---

Spelling "there" as such in one spot and as "dere" in another wasn't an oversight. It didn't matter too much if dialect was exact or not, considering the stylized and characteristic music. All that was required was a suggestion of regional flavor; and if the artist preferred—for personal literacy or racial righteousness—to enunciate any words formally rather than colloquially, that was all right.

Some years ago when Goddard Lieberson of Columbia Records informed me he had decided to issue a six-side LP of the opera, I asked to be allowed to change some opprobrious terms in the recitatives—there were about twenty—to substitutes inoffensive to the ear of today. Lieberson heartily concurred, and I spent two days going through the 559 pages of the vocal score to make the changes. (Little by little, words like "wop," "kike," and "nigger" are disappearing from print and speech—but I do believe that a few recording artists and other well-intentioned persons are nicenellying it a bit when they at times insist on elevating dialect grammar to Johnsonian heights.)

*      *      *

I was in my brother's apartment when the team of Buck and Bubbles (Ford L. Buck played Mingo) was chosen for *Porgy and Bess*. They were to go on a vaudeville tour for several months before rehearsals started. George asked their agent where they would be playing in about six weeks from that afternoon. On learning the itineraried city, George told them the vocal score would be printed by that time and he would forward a copy to the theater there so they could study up on their roles. When they returned to New York, George asked if they now had a good idea of their parts. "No, sir!" "Didn't you get a copy of the score?" "Yes, sir," said Bubbles, "I handed it to Buck and said: 'Can we learn this?' " The pages were flipped, the score hefted; then it was ruefully decided they couldn't. They thought the entire 559 pages were their parts.

*      *      *

George loved the telegram (I still have it) this talented team sent him opening night: "MAY THE CURTAIN FALL WITH THE BANG OF SUCCESS FOR YOU AS THE SUN RISES IN THE SUNSHINE OF YOUR SMILE BUCK AND BUBBLES."

83

# The Importunate Male

*"Oh, Lady, Be Good!"*

*"Put Me to the Test"*

*"I've Got a Crush on You"*

*"Nice Work If You Can Get It"*

*"I Can't Get Started"*

# OH, LADY, BE GOOD!

LADY, BE GOOD! (1924). Music, George Gershwin. "Slow and gracefully." Walter Catlett, as breezy lawyer J. Watterson Watkins, to a flock of flappers.

### 1

Listen to my tale of woe,
It's terribly sad, but true:
All dressed up, no place to go,
Each ev'ning I'm awf'ly blue.
I must win some winsome miss;
Can't go on like this.
I could blossom out, I know,
With somebody just like you.
So—

### Refrain

Oh, sweet and lovely lady, be good.
Oh, lady, be good to me!
I am so awf'ly misunderstood,
So, lady, be good to me.
Oh, please have some pity—
I'm all alone in this big city.
I tell you
I'm just a lonesome babe in the wood,
So, lady, be good to me.

---

"Oh, Lady, Be Good!" was written for a show whose working title was *Black-Eyed Susan*. At one of our pre-rehearsal conferences, when librettists Bolton and Thompson heard this song, they decided to jilt *Susan* and to call the show *Lady, Be Good!*

Usually, though, when the title of a song is identical with the title of the property it's in, the song has taken its title from the larger work. Early in the talkies the producer of a musical invariably hoped for a title song which would publicize his offering. This practice grew to such an extent that many songs with improbable titles—e.g., "Woman Disputed, I Love You"—were published. Although some in this category had quality and were successful, many were so obviously written just for hopeful box-office returns that title-song overproduction soon followed the law of diminishing returns. And for several years listeners' eardrums weren't titillated by titular tune. However, this aspect of song-writing has made a strong comeback. In recent years several songs named after their parental properties have won Academy Awards.

*     *     *

*Transatlantic Transformation.* When songs are translated for foreign publication, they frequently undergo strange metamorphoses. "Oh, Lady, Be Good!" for instance (Deutscher Text von Fritz Rotter und Otto Stransky) became:

> Was will denn bloss der Otto von dir,
> Was will er von dir bei Nacht!
> Er war bei dir bis dreiviertel Vier.
> Was hat er bei dir gemacht?

which, roughly, I'm told, means: "What did Otto exactly want of you until a quarter of four this morning?"

A somewhat nearer approach, because it at least had a repetitive sound like the original, was the translation into German (by Richard Rillo) of "Do, Do, Do." "Oh, do, do, do" became *"Der Pa-pa-pa"* and "done, done, done" was better-halfed to *"die Ma-ma-ma";* and both parents are *"bös,* Baby!" In the second line *"bös,* Baby" rhymes with *"nervös,* Baby." So, roughly, the first two lines

88

translate: "Father and mother are pretty much at odds with each other, Baby; father makes mother quite nervous, Baby."

If at times translated song lyrics seem too unrelated or tangential to the original, it's undoubtedly because many of our idioms and phrasings are untranslatable, especially with the restriction of unalterable musical themes. Imagine having to translate into Arabic or Senegalese, songs like "Flat Foot Floogie, with a Floy, Floy" or "Plant You Now, Dig You Later."

# PUT ME TO THE TEST

COVER GIRL (1944). Music, Jerome Kern. Verse: *"Poco parlando"*; burthen: "Not fast." Gene Kelly tries out part of the number on a dummy in a dress shop; then, with courage up, addresses it to Rita Hayworth.

The days of the good old knights are gone,
But chivalry still carries on.
I wear no armor,
But to my charmer
I hereby pledge my all.
In other words, I'm at your beck and call.

### Burthen 1

Put me to the test,
And I'll climb you the highest mountain,
Or swim you Radio City Fountain.
Put me to the test,
And I'll get you a queen's tiara,
Or a pyramid from the hot Sahara.
I'll be your Vic Jordan,
Red Ryder, Flash Gordon—
(With me it never rains but it pours!)
Put me to the test,
Lady, just make your request;
And an-y-thing that you de-sire is yours!

### Burthen 2

Put me to the test,
And I'll bag you a mountain puma,
Or dig you treasure of Montezuma.
Put me to the test,
And I'll ride you the Derby winner,
Or I'll pilot you to Paree for dinner.

## The Importunate Male

            It'll be a trifle
            To jump off the Eiffel—
    If that is what my lady adores.
            Put me to the test,
            Lady, just make your request;
    And an-y-thing that you de-sire is yours!

### From the Patter

    Test me—put me on my mettle!
    How would you like a snowball from Popocatepetl?
    Get you a movie contract—Goldwyn or Darryl;
    For you I'd jump Niag'ra Falls in a barrel!
    Test me—put me on my mettle!
    I can give out with Hansel if you give out with
            Gretel.
    How's about a blossom from the base of Fujiyama?
    It's yours if I have to swim from here to Yokohama.
            Anything that you suggest is yours;
            Anything that you request is yours.

---

*Time-saver.* When my brother's and my fourteen-week contract was up on *Damsel in Distress* we let the studio have two additional songs—"Pay Some Attention to Me" and "Put Me to the Test"—these in case one or two of the other songs didn't work out in filming. It turned out that nothing additional was needed vocally; but music for a dance spot was, and the tune of "Put Me to the Test" fitted. So its unused lyric reverted to me.

One day six years later I mentioned this pseudo-bravado lyric to Kern as a possible notion to fool around with for the Gene Kelly role in *Cover Girl*. Jerry thought it likely, so I managed to dig up a studio photostat of the song for him—perhaps the title or a line would give him a start for a tune. Two days later he telephoned me to hurry over—another *Cover Girl* song had been completed. I was there in a few minutes (we were neighbors—only a block and a half separated our houses); and, to my pleased

91

surprise, listened to a completely new setting for the lyric with not a word changed. What Jerry had done was follow the original musical rhythms and come up with an entirely new tune, thus saving us both a lot of work experimenting with any tangential approach to the idea.

\*     \*     \*

Not having kept up with the comic strips for some time, I'm not certain if the valorous actions of benefactors Vic Jordan, Red Ryder, and Flash Gordon are still being pictured. It's probable, though, that they and their thwarting of injustice still carry on daily and Sundays, since most syndicated comic-strip characters seem to have the perdurability ascribed to Bulgarians when I was a kid.

# I'VE GOT A CRUSH ON YOU

TREASURE GIRL (1928). Music, George Gershwin. "Gaily."
Clifton Webb and Mary Hay. (In *Strike Up the Band*, Gordon
Smith and Doris Carson.)

*Timothy*

How glad the many millions
Of Annabelles and Lillians
 Would be
 To capture me.
But you had such persistence
You wore down my resistance;
 I fell—
 And it was swell.

*Anne*

You're my big and brave and handsome Romeo.
How I won you I shall never, never know.

*Timothy*

It's not that you're attractive—
But oh, my heart grew active
 When you
 Came into view.

*Refrain*

I've got a crush on you,
 Sweetie Pie.
All the day and nighttime
 Hear me sigh.
I never had the least notion
That I could fall with so much emotion.

Could you coo,
Could you care
For a cunning cottage we could share?
The world will pardon my mush
'Cause I've got a crush,
My baby, on you.

*Anne*

I've got a crush on you,
Sweetie Pie.
All the day and nighttime
Hear me sigh.
This isn't just a flirtation:
We're proving that there's predestination.

I could coo,
I could care
For that cunning cottage we could share.
Your mush I never shall shush
'Cause I've got a crush,
My baby, on you.

---

*A Wiley Change* or *Hot Tune into Ballad*. I can't recall now why *Treasure Girl's* "Crush on You" was interpolated in the revised version of *Strike Up the Band,* since there was so much new material on hand for the latter. Anyway, although the song was a pleasant enough number in its original setting as done by Clifton Webb and Mary Hay, it was sung in *S.U.T.B.* at a faster tempo by Gordon Smith and Doris Carson—and then danced to by them at about the fastest ²⁄₄ I ever heard. So for many years I thought of this song as one exceedingly hot. Then one day I bought a then new Lee Wiley album which included the first recording of this number. I listened awhile, and wondered what the girl was up to. Fast and furious "Crush" had become slow, sentimental, and ballady. After a third playing, though, I liked the new interpretation.

And apparently so did many others, because I have yet to hear since a rendition other than the slowed-up, sentimental one.

*     *     *

*Pet Names.* Many a swain dreams up a special term of endearment for his inamorata; likewise, she for him. Generally, though, the more familiar everyday pet names are availed of. Therefore also in colloquial lyric-writing. In good standing are terms such as "dear," "honey," "ducky," "doll," "baby," "baby doll," and a score of others. In 'Crush on You" I used "sweetie pie," which I felt wasn't too diabetic a term. And I have gone for "sweet" as a noun of endearment several times. But the parent of the last two, "sweetheart" (which goes back about eight centuries to "swete heorte"), I have somehow always given a wide berth.

# NICE WORK IF YOU CAN GET IT

A DAMSEL IN DISTRESS (1937). Music, George Gershwin.
"Smoothly." Sung by Fred Astaire and a female trio at a party in
Totleigh Castle.

The man who lives for only making money
Lives a life that isn't necessarily sunny;
Likewise the man who works for fame—
There's no guarantee that time won't erase his name.
     The fact is
The only work that really brings enjoyment
Is the kind that is for girl and boy meant.
Fall in love—you won't regret it.
That's the best work of all—if you can get it.

*Refrain*

Holding hands at midnight
    'Neath a starry sky . . .
Nice work if you can get it,
And you can get it—if you try.

Strolling with the one girl,
    Sighing sigh after sigh . . .
Nice work if you can get it,
And you can get it—if you try.

Just imagine someone
    Waiting at the cottage door,
Where two hearts become one . . .
    Who could ask for anything more?

Loving one who loves you,
    And then taking that vow . . .
Nice work if you can get it,
And if you get it—Won't You Tell Me How?

## The Importunate Male

Somewhere, long ago, I read an illustrated article about a number of cartoons rejected by the humorous weeklies—cartoons and drawings not for the family trade. One, submitted to *Punch*, I think, was—I'm pretty sure—by George Belcher, whose crayon specialized in delineating London's lowly. In this one, two charwomen are discussing the daughter of a third, and the first says she's heard that the discussee 'as become an 'ore. Whereat the second observes it's nice work if you can get it. And that's all I remember about this title. It's all pretty vague and, on further reflection, it could be that I'm all wrong and that the phrase was around before I ever saw the Belcher two-liner. Anyway—

*As I See It: Q.E.D. It.* In lyric-writing it's nice work when you get hold of a seemly title, for that's half the battle. But what follows must follow through in the verse and refrain, whether the development is direct or oblique. In brief:

> A title
> Is vital.
> Once you've it—
> *Prove* it.

# I CAN'T GET STARTED

ZIEGFELD FOLLIES OF 1936. Music, Vernon Duke. "In strict tempo"; then: "Gracefully." Street corner, midnight. Bob Hope and Eve Arden in evening clothes. She is noticeably bored by his attentions. Now and then she hails a passing taxi, but none stops.

*He*

Wasn't it a wonderful dinner?

*She*

Oh, all right, not bad. Well, good night, and thanks. I'll run along now. Taxi!

*He*

Wasn't it funny how I was recognized? You know, I had to sign over twenty autographs.

*She*

That's nice. Well, good night. Taxi!

*He*

Gosh, I can't seem to get to first base with you. Good God, gal, what's wrong with me?

*She*

I wouldn't know. You, perhaps?

*He*

On six continents and seven oceans I'm tops. Everyone's crazy about me, and I'm crazy about you. I love you, want you, need you.

*She*

Hey, taxi!

## The Importunate Male

### He

I'm a glum one; it's explainable:
I met someone unattainable.
　　　Life's a bore,
The world is my oyster no more.
All the papers, where I led the news
With my capers, now will spread the news:
　　　"Superman
Turns Out to Be Flash in the Pan."

### Refrain

I've flown around the world in a plane;
I've settled revolutions in Spain;
　　The North Pole I have charted,
　　But can't get started with you.

Around a golf course I'm under par,
And all the movies want me to star;
　　I've got a house, a show-place—
　　But I get *no* place with you.

　　　You're so supreme,
　　Lyrics I write of you;
　　　Scheme
　　Just for a sight of you;
　　　Dream
　　Both day and night of you,
　　And what good does it do?

When J. P. Morgan bows, I just nod;
*Green Pastures* wanted me to play God.
　　But you've got me down-hearted
　　'Cause I can't get started with you.

### She

Oh well, what can I lose?

(*With no taxi in sight, she sighs resignedly and kisses him lightly. Whereupon he grabs her and plants a long, solid kiss as, gradually, she warms up and clutches him as closely as he her. Finally she comes up, gasping for air, and exclaims:*)

Heavens! You're wonderful! Just marvelous! Marvelous!

*He*

That's all I wanted to know. Well, good night.
     (*Blackout as he leaves her and walks off jauntily.*)

---

Vernon played me this tune and told me it had had a lyric called "Face the Music with Me"; that nothing had happened to that version; that the tune was free and I could write it up if I liked it. I liked it and wrote it up. However, there is seemingly no end of lines for "I Can't Get Started." Besides the original version for Hope and Arden (which I have here telescoped into one refrain—there were three), a radio version avoiding proper names was requested by my publisher. After that, I was asked to write a version for a possible recording by Bing Crosby, here again avoiding wherever possible the proper noun. Then there was a request for a female version to be recorded by Nancy Walker. All in all, I have fooled around with many, many lines for this piece. The sheet-music sale of the song never amounted to much (I would say that in more than twenty years it has totaled less than forty thousand copies), but an early recording by Bunny Berrigan—considered by jazz devotees a sort of classic in its field—may have been a challenge (or incentive) for the great number of recordings that have followed. Not a year has gone by, in the past fifteen or so, that up to a dozen or more new recordings haven't been issued.

# The Importunate Female

*"I Can't Get Started"*

*"Sing Me Not a Ballad"*

*"Gotta Have Me Go with You"*

*"Someone to Watch over Me"*

# I CAN'T GET STARTED

## (Female Version)

I'm a glum one; it's explainable:
I met someone unattainable.
        Life's a bore,
The world is my oyster no more.
All the papers, where I led the news
With my capers, now will spread the news:
        "Super Gal
Is Punchy and Losing Morale!"

*First Refrain*

When I sell kisses at a bazaar,
The wolves line up from nearby and far;
   With kings I've à la carted—
   But can't get started with you.

The millionaires I've had to turn down
Would stretch from London to New York Town;
   The upper crust I visit,
   But say, what *is* it—with you?

        When first we met—
How you elated me!
        Pet!
You devastated me!
        Yet—
Now you've deflated me
Till you're my Waterloo.

103

Though beauty columns ask my advice,
Though I was "Miss America" twice,
   Still you've got me outsmarted
   'Cause I can't get started with you.

*Second Refrain*

The Himalaya Mountains I climb;
I'm written up in *Fortune* and *Time*.
   I dig the 4th Dimension,
   But no attention from you!

There's always "Best regards and much love"
From Mr. Dewey—you know, the Gov;
   I'm there at ev'ry State Ball
   But behind the 8-ball with you.

      Oh, tell me why
   Am I no kick to you—
        I,
   Who'd always stick to you,
        Fly—
   Through thin and thick to you?
   Tell me why I'm taboo!

The market trembles when I sell short;
In England I'm presented at court.
   The Siamese Twins I've parted—
   But I can't get started with you.

# SING ME NOT A BALLAD

THE FIREBRAND OF FLORENCE (1945). Music, Kurt Weill. *"Allegretto amoroso."* Entrance song of the Duchess of Florence. Sung from a sedan chair by Lotte Lenya.

I am not like Circe,
Who showed men no mercy;
Men are most important in my life.
Venus, Cleo, Psyche
Are melodies in my key;
They knew how to live the high life.
Gallantry I find archaic,
Poetry I find prosaic.
Give me the man who's strong and silent:
Inarticulate—but vi'lent.

*Refrain*

Sing me not a ballad,
Send me not a sonnet.
I require no ballad:
Rhyme and time are wasted on it.

Save your books and flowers;
They're not necessaries.
Oh, the precious hours
Lost in grim preliminaries!

Deck me not in jewels;
Sigh me not your sighs;
Duel me no duels;
And—please don't vocalize.

Romance me no romances;
Treasure not my glove.
Spare me your advances—
Just, oh just make love!
Spare me your advances—
Just, oh just make love!

---

For the first entrance of the Duchess, we had a little page walk across the stage intoning to a rather bizarre melody:

Make way for the Duchess—
For Her Grace, the Duchess—
Make way for the Duchess—
For the regal, legal Duchess!

When we had to face the writing of a solo song for the Duchess, Kurt wondered what sort of melodic mood should be striven for. The page's little sing-song had echoed many times in my mind, and I suggested that its first line of ascending notes seemed a theme that could be developed into a refrain. Kurt thought this a good idea and, using the six notes of the first line, evolved this full and distinctive melody.

\*　　\*　　\*

*"I Suggested."* Whether to Kurt or George or others, there must be, without counting, at least half a dozen uses of "I suggested" among my "informative annotations." These aren't put in for any credit-claiming purposes. If, once in a great while in deliberations with the composer, a short musical phrase came to me as a possibility and was found acceptable to my collaborator, that didn't make me a composer. More often than not, as in "Sing Me Not a Ballad," my suggestion arose from some musical phrase of the composer's own, which he had overlooked or whose potentiality he was unaware of. Example 2:

## The Importunate Female

Sometime in the middle Twenties my brother and I spent three weeks or so with librettist Herbert Fields on a musical to be called *The Big Charade*. I forget now why this project was dropped. Anyhow, we did some work on it, including a pseudo-medieval march called "Trumpets of Belgravia." Years later, when *Of Thee I Sing* was being written, my brother was dissatisfied with several starts he had made for the opening—a political-campaign marching theme which inevitably had to be titled "Wintergreen for President." One day, out of the blue, I found myself humming these seven syllables to the exact rhythm and tune of the cast-behind "Trumpets of Belgravia, /Sing ta-ra, ta-ra, ta-ra. . . ." When I suggested this tune to its composer, his approval was non-verbal but physical. He immediately went to the piano and "Trumpets of Belgravia" became the serendipitous musical start of "Wintergreen for President."

Conclusion? The lyricist needn't be a musician, but if he is musically inclined he can sometimes be of help to the composer. (Not that the composer can't be of help with suggestions to the lyricist, but, in my experience, alas, rarely. Really.)

# GOTTA HAVE ME GO WITH YOU

A STAR IS BORN (1954). Music, Harold Arlen. "Steadily—
with much excitement." Sung by Judy Garland as girl vocalist
Esther Blodgett (later movie star Vicki Lester) at a benefit in the
Shrine Auditorium, Los Angeles.

What a spot, this—
Not so hot, this!
Hey, there—shy one,
Come be my one!
Please don't rush off—
Want no brush-off.
I can't compel you
To buy what I'd sell you . . .
But I've got to tell you
Like so:

*Refrain*

You wanna have bells that'll ring?
You wanna have songs that'll sing?
You want your sky a baby blue?
You gotta have me go with you!

Hey, you fool, you—
Why so cool, you,
When I'm ready
To go steady?

You wanna have eyes that'll shine?
You wanna have grapes on the vine?
You want a love that's truly true?
You gotta have me go with you!

Why the hold-out?
Have you sold out?
Time you woke up,
Time you spoke up!

## The Importunate Female

This line I'm handing you is not a handout;
As a team we'd be a standout.

You wanna live high on a dime?
You wanna have two hearts in rhyme?
Gotta have me go with you all the time!

---

Composer Arlen is no thirty-two-bar man. As one of the most individual of American show-composers he is distinctive in melodic line and unusual construction ("Black Magic," seventy-two bars; "One for My Baby," forty-eight bars; "The Man That Got Away," sixty-two bars). "Gotta" is unusual not only in its twenty-four-bar verse and forty-eight-bar refrain but also in that the first eight bars of the verse music are introduced twice in the refrain.

When inspiration or something else worth-while hits Arlen, it is rarely a complete tune. It may be a fragment of only two bars or twelve—but it is the beginning of something at some time worth mulling over, and onto an envelope or into a notebook it goes. These snatches or possible themes he calls "jots." Frequently when collaborating with him the lyricist—whether Koehler or Mercer or Harburg or myself—finds himself wondering if a resultant song isn't too long or too difficult or too mannered for popular consumption. But there's no cause for worry. Many Arlen songs do take time to catch on, but when they do they join his impressive and lasting catalogue.

# SOMEONE TO WATCH OVER ME

OH, KAY! (1926). Music, George Gershwin. *"Scherzando."* A Long Island drawing-room. Gertrude Lawrence, alone on stage, meditates musically. Stooping to conquer, she has disguised herself as a housemaid. Actually, she is the sister of a duke—all this a not unusual involvement in the Jazz Age.

> There's a saying old
> > Says that love is blind.
> Still, we're often told
> > "Seek and ye shall find."
> So I'm going to seek a certain lad I've had in mind.
> Looking ev'rywhere,
> > Haven't found him yet;
> He's the big affair
> > I cannot forget—
> Only man I ever think of with regret.
> I'd like to add his initial to my monogram.
> Tell me, where is the shepherd for this lost lamb?

> *Refrain*
>
> There's a somebody I'm longing to see:
> > I hope that he
> > Turns out to be
> Someone who'll watch over me.

> I'm a little lamb who's lost in the wood;
> > I know I could
> > Always be good
> To one who'll watch over me.

> Although he may not be the man some
> Girls think of as handsome,
> > To my heart he'll carry the key.

## The Importunate Female

Won't you tell him, please, to put on some speed,
Follow my lead?
Oh, how I need
Someone to watch over me.

---

*The Tune.* As originally conceived by the composer, this tune would probably not be around much today. At the piano in its early existence it was fast and jazzy, and undoubtedly I would have written it up as another dance-and-ensemble number. One day, for no particular reason and hardly aware of what he was at, George started and continued it in a comparatively slow tempo; and half of it hadn't been sounded when both of us had the same reaction: this was really no rhythm tune but rather a wistful and warm one —to be held out until the proper stage occasion arose for it.

*The Title.* Here and there among the notes in this book are a number of references to, and experiences and experiments with, song titles—matters such as their importance, their elusiveness, their non-copyrightability, the use of the colloquial phrase (or its paraphrase), the dummy title, the title-song title, &c. And one will gather that suitable titles are usually not easily come by, especially when a lyric is to be imposed on music already set. The following, however, will be a paragraph on "The Easiest Way to a Song Title."

George and I were well along with the score for *Oh, Kay!* when one morning at six a.m. I was rushed to Mt. Sinai Hospital for an emergency appendectomy. I was there six weeks—this was long before the antibiotics shortened stays. When, after great insistence ("They're waiting for me to finish the lyrics!"), exit was finally permitted, I was still weak but able to work afternoons. Then, with rehearsals nearing, and myself a bit behind schedule, a friend and many-faceted talent, Howard Dietz, showed up one day and offered to help out, and did. We collaborated on two lyrics and he was helpful on a couple of others. Also, one day when he heard the slowed-up ex-jazz tune he ad-libbed several titles, one of which stuck with me and which, some days later, I decided to write up.

111

And that's how it happens that this song is titled "Someone to Watch over Me." And that's: "The Easiest Way to a Song Title."

*     *     *

*The Not-Impossible He and I.F.D.* "The Man I Love," "Looking for a Boy," and "Someone to Watch over Me" and, of course, countless songs and poems of similar sentiment through the ages are more or less simple expressions of youthful daydreaming. Nonetheless:

A treatise on popular song lyrics by semanticist S. I. Hayakawa in the quarterly *ETC* (Winter 1955) has a good word for the realistic approach of songs in the "blues repertory": e.g., Eddie Green's "A Good Man Is Hard to Find." But he deeply deplores the emotional effect on listeners of such songs as "The Man I Love," the Rodgers-Hart "My Heart Stood Still" and "Blue Room," the Whiting-Donaldson "My Blue Heaven," the Johnny Black "Paper Doll," and many others. The "literary slop" in these songs and their like saddens Mr. H. because they doom us to what speech-pathologist Wendell Johnson has named "the IFD disease": I for "Idealization (the making of impossible and ideal demands upon life)"; F for "Frustration (as the result of the demands not being met), which in turn leads to Demoralization." The final step? D—demoralization or "Disorganization"—leads "into a symbolic world . . ." and "the psychiatric profession classifies this retreat as schizophrenia. . . ."

An excerpt quoted from the first-mentioned corruptive lyric: "Every night I dream a little dream, /And of course Prince Charming is the theme. . . ." One is warned that this sort of romantic whimwham builds up "an enormous amount of unrealistic idealization—the creation in one's mind, as the object of love's search, a dream 'girl (or dream boy) the fleshly counterpart of which never existed on earth." Sooner or later, unhappily, the girl chances on a Mr. Right who, in turn, is certain she 'is Miss Inevitable; and, both being under the influence of "My Heart Stood Still" (which even advocates love at first sight), they are quickly in each other's arms, taxiing to City Hall for a marriage license. On the way he sings "Blue Room" to her—she, "My Blue Heaven" to him. But, alas, this enchanted twosome is wholly unaware of the costs of rent, furniture, food, dentist, doctor, diaper service, and other necessities. There is no indication in the vocalizing "that, having found the dream-girl or dream-man, one's problems are just beginning. Rather . . . *all* problems are solved." It naturally follows that soon the marriage won't work out, when "disenchantment, frustration" and "self-pity" set in. Shortly after, they buy paper dolls, not for each other, but ones they can call their own. This comfort is, however, temporary. Subsequently, he, helpless, is in the gutters of Skid Row; she, hopeless, in a mental institution.

This is the case history of just one couple, but typical. There are millions more through whose ears infiltrate the airings of Broadway's demoniac love potions. Thus, with the continuous dinning of so-called sentimental song strength-sapping us, eventually we must become an enfeebled nation, paralyzed by IFD. Q.E.D.

# A Quartet of Trios

*"These Charming People"*

*"Don't Be a Woman If You Can"*

*"Weekend in the Country"*

*"The Cozy Nook Trio"*

# THESE CHARMING PEOPLE

TIP-TOES (1925). Music, George Gershwin. *"p-f, a tempo."* The Kayes, two uncles and a niece, a vaudeville trio stranded in Palm Beach. Influenced by the environment, they decide to go posh. Hen Kaye, Harry Watson, Jr.; Al Kaye, Andrew Tombes; "Tip-Toes" Kaye, Queenie Smith.

1

*Hen*

We must make it our ambition
To live up to our position
As we take our places in society.

*Al*

When those million dollar blokes pass,
I will never make a faux pas;
I will show them I am full of pedigree.

*"Tip-Toes"*

And the lady isn't born yet
Who can beat me at a lorgnette,
When I'm honoring the op'ra at the Met.

*All*

So if you're not social winners,
Don't invite us to your dinners—
We must warn you we'll be awful hard to get.

*Refrain*

We'll be like These Charming People,
    Putting on the ritz,
    Acting as befits
These charming people:
    Very debonair,
    Full of savoir-faire.
I hear that Mrs. Whoozis
    Created quite a stir:
She built a little love-nest
    For her and her chauffeur.
If these people can be charming,
Then we can be charming, too!


2

*Hen*

Please recall, if you've forgotten,
That my father was in cotton,
And my family is truly F.F.V.


*Al*

Merely social climbing varmints!
*Ours* was made in undergarments,
So you see before you one who's B.V.D.


*"Tip-Toes"*

If fhat's pedigree, enjoy it!
My old man came from Detroit,
So I'll have you know that I am F.O.B.


*All*

In our veins there runs the true blood!
When we mingle with the blue blood,
The Four Hundred will become Four Hundred Three.

118

## A Quartet of Trios

*Refrain*

We'll be like These Charming People,
 Putting on the ritz,
 Acting as befits
These charming people:
 Very debonair,
 Full of savoir-faire.
It seems that Mr. Smythe-Smythe
 Had no children, till
Some twenty-seven turned up
 To listen to the will.
If these people can be charming,
Then we can be charming, too!

---

I was scared stiff when tackling my first Broadway show, *Two Little Girls in Blue* (not that I ever learned to relax any time later on a job, whether a complete score or a single interpolation). However, I managed to survive and turn out a passable set of lyrics to the lively music of Vincent Youmans, with one song, "Oh, Me, Oh, My, Oh, You," becoming quite popular. (I kept hoping, though, no listener would particularly notice that among the various lyrics there were three uses of the "tender—surrender" rhyme.)

For about three years after that I worked with half a dozen composers and was able to have ten or twelve numbers interpolated in about as many shows and revues. Only two of these songs earned anything to speak of or deposit: "When All Your Castles Come Tumbling Down" (music by Milton Schwarzwald) and "Stairway to Paradise."

Then came *Lady, Be Good!*, a hit show with a generally admired score. Delighted of course with its success and the $300 or so royalty each week, I was still not completely satisfied with my contribution. I had adequately fitted some sparkling tunes, and several singable love songs and rhythm numbers had resulted. Yet I was a bit bothered by there being no lyric I considered comic.

A year later, with *Tip-Toes,* I chose to believe there had been some development in craftsmanship. *Tip-Toes* contained longer openings, many of the songs had crisp lines, and the first-act finale carried plot action for four or five minutes. And I liked the trio "These Charming People," which seemed to amuse the audience. Up to then I'd often wondered if I could do a comedy trio like the ones P. G. Wodehouse came up with—"Bongo on the Congo" from *Sitting Pretty,* for instance.

*       *       *

*A Small Summing Up.* Given a fondness for music, a feeling for rhyme, a sense of whimsy and humor, an eye for the balanced sentence, an ear for the current phrase, and the ability to imagine oneself a performer trying to put over the number in progress—given all this, I still would say it takes four or five years collaborating with knowledgeable composers to become a well-rounded lyricist. I could be wrong about the time element—there no doubt have been lyricists who knew their business from the start—but time and experiment and experience help.

# DON'T BE A WOMAN IF YOU CAN

PARK AVENUE (1946). Music, Arthur Schwartz. An Upper-Bracket Litany sung by Mary Wickes, Marthe Errolle, and Ruth Matteson. (Naturally the lines were divided among them; *unisono,* they'd soon have been out of breath in the patters.)

In this vale of tears you're either baby boy
Or baby girl when you come on the scene.
Whichever you are you find that all is not serene.
It's tough enough to be male—
But if you're born a female
You're headed for a hideous routine.

*Refrain*

If you're born that way you have to be a woman,
But we often wonder—is it worth the while?
Your neck you break
On decisions you must make
To be beguilingly in style.

If you have a choice, don't ever be a woman,
For you'll spend your life just catering to man.
You're better off a zombie,
Or Fitch and Abercrombie—
But don't be a woman if you can. ·

Take our advice,
Don't pay the price.
Don't be a woman if you can.
(*They get into a huddle, come out of it with:*)

*Patter A*

F'rinstance—PERFUME!
Ev'ry woman using perfume
Has to worry whether her fume
Will attract the men or chase 'em off instead.

121

Shall it be Chanel or Flattery,
Sexy or Assault-and-Battery,
Innuendo, Radiant, or Dash-of-Bed?
Who knows on what adventure you're embarking
Should you use It's-Better-When-You're-Parking?
Bottles by the score unveiling,
All day long you keep inhaling—
Wond'ring which will make love burgeon:
Courtesan or Vestal Virgin,
Jezebel or Farmer's Daughter—
Which one leads 'em to the slaughter?
See-Me-Later or Narcissus,
Midnight Passion, Morning Kisses?
Worried which one will beguile 'um
Till you're fit for the asylum. . . .
AND THAT'S JUST PERFUME!
Take our advice,
Don't pay the price!
To the analyst you're driven.
It's a hell of a sex that we've been given!
Don't Be a Woman If You Can!

*Patter B*

(*another huddle—then:*)
F'rinstance—FUR COATS!
Anybody is nobody,
Just a body that is shoddy,
If she hasn't got a dozen furs to wear.
Which will sell the propaganda,
Skunk or wolf or baby panda,
Elephant or chimpanzee or polar bear?
Maybe soon you'll see advertising splashes
For a coat made of "Life with Father" 's old
mustaches.
Bring them on, the more the merrier—
Belgian Donkey, Irish Terrier.
Soon they'll have a killer-diller
Made of unborn caterpillar.

122

Shall the coats that top-to-bottom us
Be giraffe or hippopotamus?
Persian Lamb is very festive.
(Leg of lamb is more digestive!)
Looking for a skin that's wearable
Makes the live-long day unbearable. . . .
AND THAT'S JUST FUR COATS!
    Take our advice,
    Don't pay the price!
Oh, the problems are inhuman;
You'd be better off being President Truman.
Don't Be a Woman If you Can!

---

There are four patters; but because of length, two are omitted: Nail Polish and Hair-Do.

The title "Don't Be a Woman If You Can" is a paraphrase of an oft-quoted remark by a turn-of-the-century songwriter. I met Dave Clark in the early Twenties at the billiard-and-pool parlor on 52nd Street—a hangout frequented nightly by songwriters. Clark was always neatly dressed, clean-shaven, and soft-spoken, even though over the years the poor chap's brain had become disordered. He was supported by contributions from the boys and a publisher or two, but he had his dignity and definite notions on quotas, so wouldn't accept more than what he considered correct. Once when I tried offering him a dollar—others gave him more— he shook his head and took only the usual quarter. (I like to think this sum was not his measure of me as a songwriter, but that either I was a newcomer or wasn't doing too well financially.)

Despite his mental handicap, every once in a great while Dave would turn out a new song—with words somewhat Gertrude Steinish to 1905-ish music—for a show he intended calling *The All-Set Waltzette Revue*. Harry Warren still remembers several of them. One, "Lazy Lou," began its verse with:

Cotton time in Georgia
Is the name he knew the place . . .

123

and the chorus ended with:

> The echo from the valley moon
> Sounds its voice like tender tune—
> > (*a sequence of chime chords, then:*)
> He was known as Lazy Lou.

Sometimes Harry, to please Dave, would play one of the songs, and would invariably be complimented with: "You played it better than Paderewski meant it." A publisher Dave didn't take to was "a faint little man"; of another annoyer he said: "I never liked him and I always will." Once when I greeted him on 47th Street he told me he was "going down to 23rd Street to see what time it is." (All I could make of this was that the four big clocks on the Metropolitan Life Insurance tower were the ones to trust.)

Even before I knew Dave I'd heard of his liking a Broadway show and recommending it to many with: "Don't miss it if you can." Had he been around in the Forties, I doubt that he would have been displeased by my adapting his most-quoted line for use as a song title. Perhaps he might even have elevated me to the dollar-donor class.

# WEEKEND IN THE COUNTRY

THE BARKLEYS OF BROADWAY (1949). Music, Harry
Warren. "Bright and Pastoral" Trio. Josh (Fred Astaire), Dinah
(Ginger Rogers), and Ezra (Oscar Levant), striding down a
country lane.

*Josh and Dinah*

With golf and tennis 'round you
And no cares to hound you—
When Mother Nature beckons, who can decline?

*Ezra*

Till Mother Nature vetoes
The bees and mosquitoes,
Mother Nature is no mother of mine.

*Refrain*

*Josh and Dinah*

A weekend in the country—
　Trees in the orchard call.

*Ezra*

When you've examined one tree
　Then you've examined them all.

*Josh and Dinah*

A weekend in the country,
　Keeping your health at par,
As on the grassy green we frolic,
'Mid the fields of rye we rollick . . .

*Ezra*

Give me rye that's alcoholic
　Frolicking at a bar.

*Josh*

Hark, hark to the song of the bull frog!

*Dinah*

At dawn you rise up with the lark.

*Ezra*

When roosters run riot
I much prefer the quiet
Of 42nd and Park.

*Josh*

Get peppy and alive-y—

*Dinah*

Don't be a city poke.

*Ezra*

I once got poison ivy.
Shall I try for poison oak?

*Josh and Dinah*

A weekend in the country—
Glorious, there's no doubt!

*Ezra*

A weekend in the country?
What's the next train out?

---

*"Lyric."* A recent book on American usage (by Bergen and Cornelia Evans) is excellent and comprehensive. But under "lyric": "The use of the noun *lyric* for the words of a song . . . is slang." I have just given a couple of hours to half a dozen books about the theater. There have been few writers as precise as Max Beerbohm; and in *Around Theatres,* in a review written in 1904,

he uses "lyrics" for the words of songs. And the year 1900 saw the publication of Harry B. Smith's compilation, *Stage Lyrics*. (Incidentally, it's hard to believe that Harry B. Smith or anyone else could be librettist and lyricist of three hundred operettas and musicals, but I have read this was so. One reference book lists seventy-seven—probably grew tired—and added "&c.") And in an early book on Gilbert and Sullivan, Gilbert, explaining his working methods, is quoted using the word. True, these references happen to be to musical-comedy songs. But all my life I have heard the words of *any* song referred to, mostly, as "the lyric" (sometimes "the words," and on rare, flossy occasions, "the poem" or "the verses"). It would seem to me that "lyric" in connection with any song these days has gained such recognition that the term is no longer limited to shoptalk or jargon.

# THE COZY NOOK TRIO

THE FIREBRAND OF FLORENCE (1945). Music, Kurt
Weill. The *palazzo* garden in moonlight. Duke Alessandro is making a play for Cellini's model, Angela. But his passes are fraught
with apprehension, as he senses that Cellini lurks in the background. At times the sardonic latter sneaks a glance over a hedge.
Duke, Melville Cooper; Angela, Beverly Tyler; Cellini, Earl
Wrightson.

1

*Duke*

Dear young woman, when I'm gazing
Fondly at you, it's amazing
   How much love I'd love to vow.
But though I've had a lot of practice
At this sort of thing, the fact is
   I am not myself just now.

*Angela*

Dear my lord, I fear you're scoffing.

*Duke*

With Cellini in the offing,
   I'm as nervous as can be.

*Angela*

Your highness—

*Duke*

      Call me Bumpy.

*Angela*

You do seem rather jumpy.

*Duke*

I beg you bear with me.

## A Quartet of Trios

### Refrain

I know where there's a nosy cook—

### Angela

My lord, you mean a cozy nook?

### Duke

Yes, yes, of course! A cozy nook for two.
And there we two can kill and boo.

### Angela

My lord, you mean we'll bill and coo?

### Cellini

It seems to me that killing and booing should do.

### Duke

I cannot promise bedding wells.

### Angela

My thoughts were not on wedding bells.

### Duke

Whatever I do is for the fatherland;
And so I love your sturgeon vile.

### Angela

My lord, you mean my virgin style?

### Duke

It's wonderful how love can understand!

### 2

### Duke

Listen, loveliest of your gender:
Somehow, phrases soft and tender
Do not sound their best tonight.

129

*Angela*

It seems you get the words all twisted.

*Duke*

But the way that you assisted
   Thrills me through with sheer delight.

*Angela*

When the ducal throat is vocal,
Women from afar, or local,
   Always know what's on his mind.

*Cellini*

The situation vexes;
I'm finding out that sex is
   The curse of humankind.

*Refrain*

*Duke*

I know where there's a booden wench—

*Angela*

My lord, you mean a wooden bench?

*Duke*

Yes, yes, of course! A wooden bench for two.
And there we two can biss a kit.

*Angela*

My lord, you mean we'll kiss a bit?

*Cellini*

He may be biting more biss-a-kit than he can chew!

*Angela*

How masterf'ly you stress your puit!
I mean the way you press your suit;
I sense it from the way you press my hand.

130

## A Quartet of Trios

*Duke*

And so I offer wedless bliss.

*Angela*

I'd rather it were bedless wiss.

*Duke*

It's wonderful how love can understand.

---

More than thirty years ago, in *Lady, Be Good!,* I tried for a number based on spoonerisms, but it never made rehearsal. This later attempt, "The Cozy Nook Trio," was, I think, not unagreeably accepted by the few who paid to see *The Firebrand of Florence,* and by the few more who came in on passes.

*Gratuitous Cultural Note.* "Spoonerism" (a form of what the professors call "metathesis") is defined as "the accidental transposition of initial letter or syllables of two or more adjacent words." These inadvertent verbal lapses are of course named after the Rev. W. A. Spooner (1844–1930) of New College, Oxford, who was given to transpositions like "Will nobody pat my hiccup?" for "Will nobody pick my hat up?"; "our queer old dean" for "our dear old queen," &c. But, although named after the good Dr., this sort of unintentional juxtaposition must have occurred countless times in the thousands of languages ever since primitive speech. Verbal speech, that is—as I can't conceive of a spoonerism in Grunt Communication. (Nor, for that matter, in African Drum, Indian Smoke Signal, Wigwag, Mirror Flash, Footsie, or any of the numerous other nonverbal languages.)

*   *   *

Two days after I wrote the above note I happened across No. 20 of the quarterly *Gentry.* An article in it, coincidentally enough, pertains to "Spoonerisms, that little trick of transposing word beginnings that was a popular form of humor in frontier days." This

131

definition introduces the reproduction of a hitherto unpublished manuscript "kept in deliberate oblivion for a hundred years." The author (a Midwest lawyer at the time) began his one-page piece of playful syllable-juggling with: "He said he was riding *bass-ackwards* on a *jass-ack* through a *patton-cotch* . . ." and there follow a dozen other examples of the twisted term—all in the handwriting of Abraham Lincoln. But it was another President, our thirty-first, who, through no slip of his own, was connected with the most-publicized syllable-switch: when radio announcer Von Zell introduced him across the country as "Hoobert Heever."

\*    \*    \*

To revert—a year later—to Spooner: I can't resist this one, thanks to a new edition of *Brewer's Dictionary:* "Yes, indeed; the Lord *is* a shoving leopard."

# A Quintet of Findings

*"Beginner's Luck"*

*"Dissertation on the State of Bliss"*

*"Love Walked In"*

*"The Search Is Through"*

*"This Is New"*

# (I'VE GOT) BEGINNER'S LUCK

SHALL WE DANCE (1937). Music, George Gershwin. "Not fast." Fred Astaire to Ginger Rogers.

> At any gambling casino
> From Monte Carlo to Reno,
> They tell you that a beginner
> Comes out a winner.
> Beginner fishing for flounder
> Will catch a seventeen-pounder.
> That's what I always heard
> And always thought absurd,
> But now I believe ev'ry word.
> For—

### Refrain

> I've got beginner's luck.
> The first time that I'm in love, I'm in love with you.
> (Gosh, I'm lucky!)
> I've got beginner's luck.
> There never was such a smile or such eyes of blue!
> (Gosh, I'm fortunate!)
> This thing we've begun
> Is much more than a pastime,
> For this time is the one
> Where the first time is the last time!
> I've got beginner's luck,
> Lucky through and through,
> 'Cause the first time that I'm in love,
> I'm in love with you.

*An Early Finding: Occupational Nuisance.* Working incommunicado, trying to solve the riddle of a lyric for a tune, I sometimes didn't get to bed until after sunrise. Even then the tune could be so persistent that it could keep running on through sleep, and was still with me at breakfast. And later in the day when I was about to tackle some other problem, it was capable of capricious intrusion with the threat of "Write me up! Work on me now or you'll never get through!" However, after some years of tussling with any number of tunes, I found that the newer ones gradually became less tenacious and more tractable. Fortunately, one develops a kind of forgettery into which they can be cast, to be permitted out and given consideration when the time is propitious or the deadline not too far off.

# DISSERTATION ON THE STATE OF BLISS

## *or*

## LOVE AND LEARN BLUES

THE COUNTRY GIRL (1954). Music, Harold Arlen. "Slow rock." Sung at a bar by Mistress of Ceremonies Jacqueline Fontaine, assisted by a somewhat swacked customer, played by Bing Crosby.

Love and learn, love and learn.
It's a breeze, then a burn.
You retreat, then return.
You may have climbed the Tree of Knowledge,
But when you love you *really* learn.

Love and learn. Learn a lot.
It's the be-and-end-all, then it's not.
It's a dream, it's a plot.
It's something out of Seventh Heaven—
Then Something Misbegot.

Each morning when I count my blessings,
They tally up to none.
I've arrived at this:
What some call bliss
Is somewhat overdone.

Love and learn. Weep and sing
Till the final day of reckoning.
But when arms start to cling,
With the thrills kisses bring—
What you have learned is,
Is:
You haven't learned a thing.

*Coda*

It's a dream and it's a plot;
What you thought it was, was not.
But when arms begin to cling,
And angels start to sing—
What you have learned is,
            Is:
You haven't learned a thing.

---

This blues was written and titled as "Love and Learn." I subsequently learned that there had been at least three songs so named, and when the creators of one of them objected, it was a simple matter to make the phrase the subtitle and to decorate the number with the rather impressive "Dissertation on the State of Bliss."

# LOVE WALKED IN

GOLDWYN FOLLIES (1938). Music, George Gershwin. "Slowly, with much expression." Sung by Kenny Baker.

Nothing seemed to matter anymore;
Didn't care what I was headed for.
Time was standing still;
Nothing counted till
There came a knock-knock-knocking at the door.

*Refrain*

Love walked right in
And drove the shadows away;
Love walked right in
And brought my sunniest day.

One magic moment,
And my heart seemed to know
That love said "Hello!"—
Though not a word was spoken.

One look, and I
Forgot the gloom of the past;
One look, and I
Had found my future at last.

One look, and I
Had found a world completely new,
When love walked in with you.

---

*High Reception.* In the late spring of '38 my wife and I were making a weekend California and Nevada automobile tour. Saturday at twilight we were rounding the top of nine-thousand-foot-high

Donner Pass when we were sideswiped by an oncoming car whose driver was higher than the Pass. Fortunately, no one was hurt, and another car offered to send us help from Truckee, a matter of waiting a couple of hours for a tow truck. We had overcoats on, but it was getting very chilly, so I said to my wife: "Let's get in the car, where it'll be warmer." We got in, turned on the radio, listened to a local commercial for a few seconds, then tried for some music and happened to get the Hit Parade. "Love Walked In" had been one of ten songs on the show for some weeks; however, since the program had just a few minutes left to go, I supposed we had missed finding out if the song was still on the list or not. But then came the announcement: "And now, the Number One Song in the country: 'Love Walked In.'" Which more than made up for a badly busted fender.

\*     \*     \*

Despite the fact that this song was one of the top ones that year, the tune, which my brother considered "Brahmsian," deserved a better lyric. There was no special plot situation for it in the *Follies* screenplay when he chose it from a number of reserve tunes kept in his notebooks. All that was required was something for the fine tenor voice of Kenny Baker. Wallowing in a swamp of vague generalities, I finally emerged with this lyric based on its ambulatory title. What particularly bothered me was the injection of "right" in "Love walked right in"—obviously a padding word. This I deleted from the title when the song was sent to the music-publisher. But my feeling about the lyric is evidently of indifference to those who like the song.

# THE SEARCH IS THROUGH

THE COUNTRY GIRL (1954). Music, Harold Arlen. Verse: "Tenderly"; chorus: "With a slow steady pulse." Bing Crosby plays Frank Elgin, a onetime musical-comedy star attempting a comeback. In a flashback we are at a recording session. The star is at the height of his career and is making a record (78 RPM) of a presumable hit song of the period.

> The flaxen hair,
> The tender voice,
> The laughing eyes . . .
> Gave me no choice.

> No more the doubt
> I used to face;
> No more the doubt—
> No more the chase.

> *Chorus*
> The search is through—
> You've got what it takes;
> There was no passing you by.

> In my *Who's Who*
> You've got what it takes:
> The Who, the Where, the When, the Why.

> One look, and oh!
> No painting I know
> Can equal your loveliness—
> Head to toe.

At last the breaks!
You've got what it takes;
So easy to see
For all time to be—
You've got what it takes
To take me.

---

If "Chorus," and not "Refrain," introduces the body of this song, the simple reason is that "Chorus" is generally the house usage in Arlen's publishing company.

In the film a flashback to the Thirties showed Crosby dubbing an imagined hit song of that period, but "The Search Is Through" was no hit in the period in which it was written—the middle Fifties. As Arlen might put it: it didn't make any noise. "Noise" in this connection is Arlen's term and has nothing to do with decibels. A "noisy" song is one that gets around, sells copies, and is recorded a good many times.

# THIS IS NEW

LADY IN THE DARK (1941). Music, Kurt Weill. "With warmth." Sung in the Second Dream Sequence by Gertrude Lawrence and Victor Mature, as Liza Elliott, magazine editor, and Randy Curtis, movie star, supported by a choir *mysterioso*.

With you I used to roam
Through The Pleasure Dome
    Of Kubla Khan.
I held you tight, my love,
In the gardens of
        Old Babylon.
I lost you through the centuries.
    I find you once again,
    And find myself the luckiest of men.

*Refrain*

This is new—
I was merely existing.
*This* is new
And I'm living at last.
    Head to toe,
You've got me so I'm spellbound;
    I don't know
If I am heaven or hell-bound.
    This is new—
Is it Venus insisting
    That I'm through
With the shadowy past?
    I am hurled
    Up to another world
    Where life is bliss,
        And this—
        Is new.

143

# A Quintet of Findings

Several actors read for the role of Randy Curtis, movie star, in *Lady in the Dark,* but none had been found satisfactory. About a week before rehearsals were to start, a friend of mine, Gene Solow, just in from California, popped in to see me at the Essex House. When I told him of our casting problem, he said that a likely prospect, Victor Mature, had been on the plane with him, but he didn't know where Victor was to stay. I was busy shaving and asked: "Would you mind calling the Hotel Pierre? Maybe he's just registered there." No Mature. "Try the Algonquin." No Mature. "21" was phoned, with the same result. "It's probably crazy—but try the hotel desk here." "Crazy, eh?" said Gene a few seconds later—"He's registering right now."

\*     \*     \*

Although the legend under "This Is New" states that the song was sung by Gertrude Lawrence and Victor Mature, actually it was finally done by Gertie alone. When handsome "hunk of man" Mature sang, his heart and the correct key weren't in it. By cutting out the verse with its "luckiest of men," we were able to give the song to Gertie and have it remain in the score.

# A Sextet of Irreverence

*"It Ain't Necessarily So"*

*"Blah, Blah, Blah"*

*"On and On and On"*

*"Stiff Upper Lip"*

*"Union Square"*

*"The Union League"*

# IT AIN'T NECESSARILY SO

PORGY AND BESS (1935). Music, George Gershwin. "With humor." Sung by John W. Bubbles as Sportin' Life.

It ain't necessarily so,
It ain't necessarily so—
  De t'ings dat yo' li'ble
  To read in de Bible—
It ain't necessarily so.

Li'l' David was small, but—oh my!
Li'l' David was small, but—oh my!
  He fought Big Goliath
  Who lay down and dieth—
Li'l' David was small, but—oh my!

Wadoo! Zim bam boddle-oo, zim bam boddle-oo!
Hoodle ah da wah da! Hoodle ah da wah da!
Scatty wah! Yeah!

Oh Jonah, he lived in de whale,
Oh Jonah, he lived in de whale—
  Fo' he made his home in
  Dat fish's abdomen—
Oh Jonah, he lived in de whale.

Li'l' Moses was found in a stream,
Li'l' Moses was found in a stream—
   He floated on water
   Till Ole Pharaoh's daughter
She fished him, she *says,* from dat stream.
Wadoo! Zim &c.
   It ain't necessarily so,
   It ain't necessarily so.
     Dey tell all you chillun
     De debble's a villun
   But 'tain't necessarily so.


   To get into hebben
   Don't snap fo' a seben—
Live clean! Don't have no fault!
   Oh, I takes dat gospel
   Whenever it's pos'ple—
But wid a grain of salt!


Methus'lah live nine hunderd years,
Methus'lah live nine hunderd years—
   But who calls dat livin'
   When no gal'll give in
To no man what's nine hunderd years?


   I'm preachin' dis sermon to show
   It ain't nessa, ain't nessa,
   Ain't nessa, ain't nessa,
   Ain't necessarily so!


     *Encore Limerick*

'Way back in 5,000 B.C.
Ole Adam an' Eve had to flee.
   Sure, dey did dat deed in
   De Garden of Eden—
But why chasterize you an' me?


148

*Dummy Title.* After my brother played me a sixteen-bar tune which he thought might be the start of something for Sportin' Life in the Picnic Scene, I asked for a lead sheet (the simple vocal line); and to remember the rhythm and accents better, I wrote across the top a dummy title—the first words that came to my mind: "It ain't necessarily so." (I could just as well have written "An order of bacon and eggs," "Tomorrow's the 4th of July," "Don't ever sell Telephone short"—anything—the sense didn't matter. All I required was a phrase which accented the second, fifth, and eighth syllables to help me remember the rhythm.)

Struggling for two days with the tune, I came up with no eurekan notion. Then I remembered I had once written a dummy title to a Vincent Youmans melody when we were working on *Two Little Girls in Blue,* and a couple of days later when Youmans asked if I had finished the song, I told him I hadn't as yet got a title. Youmans: "What do you mean? It's called 'Oh, Me, Oh, My, Oh, You.' " Me: "But that was only my dummy title." Nevertheless, Youmans insisted that he was crazy about that particular title—which was fine with me, because I couldn't think of anything else —and the song turned out to be the most popular in the show.

So I began to explore the possibilities of *this* dummy title. At one point I decided that troublemaker Sportin' Life, being among a group of religious Sons-and-Daughters-of-Repent-Ye-Saith-the-Lord picnickers, might try to startle them with a cynical and irreligious attitude. And what would certainly horrify his auditors would be his saying that some accounts in the Bible weren't necessarily so. Once I had the rhymes "Bible—li'ble" and "Goliath—dieth," I felt I was probably on the right track. George agreed. He then improvised the scat sounds, "Wa-doo, Zim bam boddle-oo." Together, in a week or so, we worked out the rather unusual construction of this piece, with its limerick musical theme, the crowd responses, the lush melodic middle, and the "ain't nessa, ain't nessa" coda. Happily, in all the years that the song has been around, I have received only one letter remarking on its possible irreverence.

*"Resistance Hymn."* During World War II *Porgy and Bess* was somehow permitted by the Nazis to be produced at the Royal

Opera House in Copenhagen. This song came "to be something like a resistance hymn in Nazi-occupied Denmark—ever since the evening when, after the grimly boastful routine broadcast of the German army's usual victory communiqué, the secret Danish underground radio had cheerfully cut in with a significant 'It Ain't Necessarily So.' . . ." (Cf. Fred M. Hechinger: "American Goods Preferred," *Harper's,* December 1950, p. 81.)

# BLAH, BLAH, BLAH

DELICIOUS (1931). Music, George Gershwin. Swedish El Brendel demonstrates to Scottish Janet Gaynor how a Theme Song is rhymed.

> I've written you a song,
>> A beautiful routine;
>>> (I hope you like it.)
> My technique can't be wrong:
>> I learned it from the screen.
>>> (I hope you like it.)
> I studied all the rhymes that all the lovers sing;
> Then just for you I wrote this little thing.

*Refrain*

> Blah, blah, blah, blah, moon,
>> Blah, blah, blah, above;
> Blah, blah, blah, blah, croon,
>> Blah, blah, blah, blah, love.
> Tra la la la, merry month of May;
> Tra la la la, 'neath the clouds of gray.
> Blah, blah, blah, your hair,
>> Blah, blah, blah, your eyes;
> Blah, blah, blah, blah, care,
>> Blah, blah, blah, blah, skies.
> Tra la la la, tra la la la la, cottage for two—
> Blah, blah, blah, blah, blah, darling with you!

---

*Another Palimpsest Melody.* Although this song didn't have a history of as many lyrics rubbed out as did, say, "Long Ago and Far Away," it did take on three different sets of words in the course of three years.

The tune was composed in 1928 for the operetta *East Is West,* and I wrote it up as a sort of Chinese invocation, titled "Lady of the Moon." But *East Is West* was called off "temporarily" by Ziegfeld and we were switched to *Show Girl*. For the new show Ziegfeld asked if I would mind collaborating with lyricist Gus Kahn, as he owed Gus a commitment. I welcomed the opportunity because *Show Girl* had to be done quickly to make a much too soon Boston opening date.

Including openings and finalettos and several songs written during rehearsal, George, Gus, and I wound up with twenty-seven musical items. Many of these were for imagined spots, as we were as vague about what most of the scenes would be as librettist William Anthony McGuire himself was. (We started rehearsals with the script for only the opening scene. Genial Bill McGuire apparently wasn't worrying much about a deadline on this one and loved listening to anything new we played him. And "You never can tell. Maybe I'll get a good idea for a scene from one of the songs.")

There was much musical entertainment in *Show Girl*. Of the twenty-seven items we wrote, fourteen were used. Then there was the ballet *An American in Paris,* which opened the second act and ran at least fifteen minutes. Then there was a scene in which Duke Ellington and his band played a couple of their numbers; and another in which Clayton, Jackson, and Durante contributed several of their own specialties. And I see by the program that singer-guitarist Nick Lucas did a few of the songs associated with him. Too, the finale of the show ("Stagedoor Ziegfeld Theatre") reprised half a dozen of our numbers. Everything considered, I wouldn't be surprised if *Show Girl* set a record for sparseness of dialogue in a musical.

One of the thirteen discarded numbers carried a new lyric to the tune of "Lady of the Moon." Sensing at the time that *East Is West* would never be produced (Ziegfeld's finances weren't what they'd been and the production costs of *East Is West* would be three times that of *Show Girl*), I salvaged the melody of the moon song, and Gus and I gave it a light ballad lyric called "I Just Looked at You." But since there was no particular use for this version either, I kept the tune in mind as a future possibility.

152

## A Sextet of Irreverence

By 1930 the Hollywood "theme song" (usually a love song) was so much in the ascendance that I thought a mild spoof on the theme-song theme wouldn't be amiss. Needing a good ballady tune, I chose the present one, and as "Blah, Blah, Blah" it emerged for the third (and last) time as a song, when it was accepted for the film *Delicious*.

# ON AND ON AND ON

LET 'EM EAT CAKE (1933). Music, George Gershwin. *"Vigo-roso"* and *"Tempo di Marcia."* Sung by a Squad of General Snook-field's Troops.

Left! Right! Left! Right!
Marching for a dream—
We sing as we go marching
And we've got a marching theme.
The theme is one that ev'ry army sings
On its way to conquer cabbages or kings.

*Refrain*

On, and on, and on!
Hither and thither—and yon!
It seems to be the thing
For marching men to sing:
"On, and on, and on!"
So—
On, and on, and on!
Hither and thither—and yon!
For movements military
There is no itinerary
Like
On, and on, and on!
ON-AND-ON-AND-ON!

## A Sextet of Irreverence

### 2

On, and on, and on!
Hither and thither—and yon!
No matter what the time
Or scenery or clime:
"On, and on, and on!"
So—
On, and on, and on—
Crossing that ole Rubicon.
No sooner do we get there
Than again this chansonnette there:
"On, and on, and on!"
ON-AND-ON-AND-ON!

\* \* \*

(*Shortly after this soldierly sentiment, General Snookfield sings:*)
I've brushed my teeth and I've washed my face,
And I've had a fine shampoo.
What more can a general do
When his troops are on review?

I've combed my hair and I've had a shave,
And my underwear is new.
What more, what more,
What more can a general do
When his troops are on review?

# STIFF UPPER LIP

A DAMSEL IN DISTRESS (1937). Music, George Gershwin. "With humor." Sung by Gracie Allen as secretary and girl friend of an American press agent, George Burns, in England.

What made Good Queen Bess
Such a great success?
What made Wellington do
What he did at Waterloo?
What makes every Englishman
A fighter through and through?
It isn't roast beef or ale or home or mother;
It's just a little thing they sing to one another:

*Refrain*

Stiff upper lip! Stout fella!
Carry on, old fluff!
Chin up! Keep muddling through!
Stiff upper lip! Stout fella!
When the going's rough—
Pip-pip to Old Man Trouble—and a toodle-oo, too!

Carry on through thick and thin
If you feel you're in the right.
Does the fighting spirit win?
Quite, quite, quite, quite, quite!

Stiff upper lip! Stout fella!
When you're in a stew—
Sober or blotto,
This is your motto:
Keep muddling through!

# A Sextet of Irreverence

## Second Refrain

Stiff upper lip! Stout fella!
Carry on, old bean!
Chin up! Keep muddling through!
Stiff upper lip! Stout fella!
Dash it all—I mean
Pip-pip to Old Man Trouble—and a toodle-oo, too!

When a bounder starts to hiss,
You must give him blow for blow.
Make the blighter cry, "What's this?
'Ullo, 'ullo, 'ullo, 'ullo, 'ullo!"

Stiff upper lip! Stout fella!
With a derring-do!
Sober or blotto,
This is your motto:
Keep muddling through!

---

*Surprise.* When I did this lyric twenty-two years ago I remembered "muddle through" as a Briticism—sometimes of criticism, sometimes of resolution—much used at the time of World War I. (Almost as prevalent as World War II's term of approval, "good show.") Then, from various characters in Wodehouse, came phrases like "pip-pip," "toodle-oo," and "stout fella." And whether Englishmen actually greeted each other or not with "old bean" or "old fluff" or "old tin of fruit" didn't matter frightfully—we had been conditioned by vaudevillians and comic weeklies to think they did.

Recently I had occasion (the occasion being this note) to look up "muddle through" and "stiff upper lip." And "muddle through" is all right: it goes back to England's statesman and orator John Bright, who used it in a speech in the 1860's. But as for my lyric's title, "Stiff Upper Lip"—I find—big surprise to me—that it's an

Americanism. The *Oxford English Dictionary* has this 1833 quote from *The Down Easters,* by American novelist John Neal: "What's the use of boo-hooin'? Keep a stiff upper lip. . . ." And *A Dictionary of Americanisms* has an even earlier quote (1815) from a Boston newspaper called *Massachusetts Spy:* "I kept a stiff upper lip. . . ." So my believing it a Briticism was wrong by the better half of a century; for according to the research of British philologist Eric Partridge, the phrase was adopted by the English only about 1880.

# UNION SQUARE

LET 'EM EAT CAKE (1933). Music, George Gershwin. Act I, scene iii. Although the groups on stage carry denunciatory placards, they sing charmingly to a schottischey strain until agitator Kruger, played by Phil Loeb, strides on.

Our hearts are in communion
When we gather down on Union
　　Square, heigh ho.
When whiskers are unshaven
One can always find a haven
　　There, heigh ho.
Though some may prefer the charming Bronnix,
　Though some sing of dainty Sutton Place,
'Tis here we discover all the tonics
　That cure all the problems of the race.
On boxes they put soap in,
How we love it in the open
　　Air, heigh ho.
We may not fill our stomics,
But we're full of economics
　　Down on Union Square,
　　Down here on Union Square.
　　　　　(*Enter Kruger and henchmen*)

*Kruger*

Conditions as they are
Cannot go very far;
The world must move and we are here to move it.
The Brotherhood of Man
Is crying for a Plan,
So here's my Plan—I know you can't improve it!

*Henchmen*

Conditions as they are
Can *not* go very far;
So—listen to his Plan
For Man.

*Kruger*

Down with one and one make two,
Down with ev'rything in view!
Down with all majorities;
Likewise all minorities!
Down with you, and you, and you!

*Ensemble*

Down with one and two make three;
Down with all of us, says he.

*Kruger*

Somehow I abominate
Anything you nominate.

*Henchmen*

Ev'rything from A,B,C to X,Y,Z.

*Kruger*

That's the torch we're going to get the flame from!
If you don't like it, why don't you go back
where you came from?

*Ensemble* (*to one another*)

If you don't like it, why don't you go back
where you came from?

160

## A Sextet of Irreverence

*Kruger* (*with repeats by Ensemble*)

Let's tear down the House of Morgan!
 House of Morgan!
Let's burn up the Roxy organ!
 Roxy organ!
Down with Curry and McCooey!
 And McCooey!
Down with chow mein and chop suey!
 And chop suey!
Down with music by Stravinsky!
 By Stravinsky!
Down with shows except by Minsky!
 Up with Minsky!

*Ensemble*

Happiness will fill our cup,
When it's "Down with ev'rything that's up!"

*Kruger*

Down with books by Dostoyevsky!
 Dostoyevsky!
Down with Boris Thomashefsky!
 Thomashefsky!
Down with Balzac! Down with Zola!
 Down with Zola!
Down with pianists who play "Nola"!
 (*All dance to opening four bars "Nola"*)
Down with all the Upper Classes!
 Upper Classes!
Might as well include the Masses!
 'Clude the Masses!
Happiness will fill our cup
When it's "Down with ev'rything that's up!"
 (*They are all pretty excited by now*)
So down with this, and down with that!
And down with ev'rything in view!
The hell with this, the hell with that!
The hell with you, and you, and you!

161

*(To one another)*

One Group

The hell with who?

Second Group

The hell with you!

Third

The hell with whom?

Fourth

The hell with youm!

*(All square off. A free-for-all follows. Policeman enters, blows whistle. The grounded ones get up, flick dust off. All, Policeman included, saunter off singing:)*

> Our hearts are in communion
> When we gather down on Union
> Square, heigh ho. &c.

---

If *Strike Up the Band* was a satire on War, and *Of Thee I Sing* one on Politics, *Let 'Em Eat Cake* was a satire on Practically Everything. Straddling no fence, it trampled the Extreme Right one moment, the Extreme Left the next. Kaufman and Ryskind's libretto was at times wonderfully witty—at other times unrelentingly realistic in its criticism of the then American scene. Possibly the following short musical speech (unused) written for professional agitator Kruger gives an indication of what *Let 'Em Eat Cake* strove for:

> Conditions as they were
> Must nevermore recur.
> Whatever is, shouldn't be;
> Whatever isn't—should.
> Whatever wasn't, will be;
> And I'm arranging it all for your good.

## A Sextet of Irreverence

Among some of the leftovers for "Union Square" I find:

Let's tear down the House and Senate!
Down with Joan and Connie Bennett!
Down with Russia, down with Stalin!
Down with four quarts to the gallon!
Down with Marx and those four brothers!
Down with plays by Rachel Crothers!

# THE UNION LEAGUE*

LET 'EM EAT CAKE (1933). Music, George Gershwin. Act I, scene v. Sumptuous Victorian library of an exclusive club. A number of well-dressed, whiskered gentlemen—octogenarian, mostly—are dozing in easy chairs. They stretch, rise slowly, and intone:

> We are members,
> Our fathers were members,
> *Their* fathers were members,
> Our great-great-great-grandfathers were members
> Of the Union League, the U-n-i-o-n League.

### Club Song

> Cloistered from the noisy city,
> Standing pat and sitting pretty,
>   We are they who represent
>   Safety First and 5%.
>
> When we wake, which is infrequent,
> We keep wond'ring where last week went;
>   Then back to our chairs we creep,
>   And we go right back to sleep.
>
> "Don't swap horses in a river!"
> "Watch your kidneys, watch your liver!"
>   That's the essence of our lives—
>   That, and New York Central 5's.
>
> Action would be suicidal;
> Rip Van Winkle is our idol:
>   He's the one man does intrigue
>   The members of the U-n-i-o-n League.

*(Exhausted, they reseat themselves, and fall asleep.)*

164

## A Sextet of Irreverence

### 2

*(Once we had the old boys asleep again, we had to let them lie.
But the following was ready, in case:)*

Window gazing, nothing rankles
When we view the charming ankles
   Of the lovely ladies who
   Ramble down the avenue.

Too, the heartbeat in us quickens
When a new book's out by Dickens.
   (Bulwer-Lytton's through and done.
   Trollope is a name we shun.)

Yearly to the bar we bustle,
Drink a toast to Lil'ian Russell—
   (Lil'ian, fairest of the fair!)
   Then we play at solitaire.

Finding this place to our liking,
We sent packing Lief the Viking.
   "Sleep and rest shall ne'er fatigue
   The members of the U-n-i-o-n League."

# Not for a Musicologist

*"By Strauss"*

*"Fascinating Rhythm"*

*"Harlem River Chanty"*

*"Mischa, Jascha, Toscha, Sascha"*

*"The Real American Folk Song"*

*"Sweet and Low-Down"*

*"That Lost Barber Shop Chord"*

*"Tschaikowsky"*

# BY STRAUSS

THE SHOW IS ON (1936). Music, George Gershwin. *"Tempo di Valse Viennoise."* Sung by Gracie Barrie.

Away with the music of Broadway!
Be off with your Irving Berlin!
 Oh, I'd give no quarter
 To Kern or Cole Porter,
And Gershwin keeps pounding on tin.
 How can I be civil
 When hearing this drivel?
It's only for night clubbing souses.
 Oh, give me the free'n'easy
 Waltz that is Viennesey—
  And, go tell the band
  If they want a hand
The waltz must be Strauss's.
  Ya, ya, ya—
  Give me Oom-pah-pah!

*Refrain*

When I want a melody
 Lilting through the house,
Then I want a melody—
  BY STRAUSS.
It laughs, it sings! The world is in rhyme,
Swinging to three-quarter time.
 Let the Danube flow along,
  And "The Fledermaus!"
 Keep the wine and give me song—
  BY STRAUSS.

> By Jo, by Jing,
> BY STRAUSS is the thing!
> So I say to Ha-cha-cha:
> Heraus!
> Just give me an Oom-pah-pah
> BY STRAUSS.

---

In New York one night in the spring of '36, stage director Vincente Minnelli was present when my brother and I were musically kidding around by exaggerating the lifts and plunges and *luftpauses* of the Viennese waltz. We had written only about half of this piece when we dropped it for something more usable. In August of that year we checked in at the Beverly Wilshire Hotel in Beverly Hills to start work on *Shall We Dance*. We were there but a few days when a telegram arrived from Vincente. In it he stated he was preparing a new Broadway revue and asked us please to work on the Straussian take-off, which he felt he could use. So we took off a day from the film for the stage take-off, finished the waltz, and airmailed it. We never saw the show, but I understand the song was acceptably presented and received.

✻   ✻   ✻

*"Extra Long Verses."* When "By Strauss" was being prepared for sheet-music publication, my brother received a letter from a concerned young woman in the editing department. She wrote that the verse was "unusually long" and "would take up at least three pages. . . . Is there anything you can suggest that would help us to get the number out in the usual amount of pages?" (Usually two.)

On 12/4/36 my brother wrote:

*Dear Selma,*

I am very sorry that the verse to BY STRAUSS is so long that it requires perhaps an extra page in the publication copy, but then it's always been my policy to give the pub-

lic a lot for their money; and I think it would be a good
idea to put on the title page—"This song has an extra
long verse so you are getting more notes per penny than
in any other song this season.". . . And even if the song
doesn't sell I would like my grandchildren (if I ever have
any) to see the trouble that their grand-daddy took with
verses. In other words, dear Selma, I would like the song
printed as I wrote it, with no commas left out.

> *Love and kisses,*
> GEORGE

*   *   *

When the song was to be included in the score of *An American
in Paris* (under Vincente Minnelli's movie direction this time),
MGM's legal department said clearances would have to be se-
cured from Berlin and Porter and the Kern estate for use of the
names. Which probably could have been easily acquired, but it
was less bothersome to write new lines.

I wrote several variants for the opening of the verse. This is
the one that was chosen for the film:

> The waltzes of Mittel Europa—
> They're mellow and warm you within,
>     While each day discloses
>     What Broadway composes
> Is emptiness pounding on tin.
>     How can I be civil &c.

One discarded:

> Beware of that popular music!
> In dynamite danger must lurk.
>     You hear in an awed way
>     The music of Broadway
> And suddenly you go berserk.
>     How can I be civil &c.

171

# FASCINATING RHYTHM

LADY, BE GOOD! (1924). Music, George Gershwin. "With agitation." Fred and Adele Astaire, assisted by Ukulele Ike.

Got a little rhythm, a rhythm, a rhythm
That pit-a-pats through my brain;
So darn persistent,
The day isn't distant
When it'll drive me insane.
Comes in the morning
Without any warning,
And hangs around me all day.
I'll have to sneak up to it
Someday, and speak up to it.
I hope it listens when I say:

*Refrain*

Fascinating Rhythm,
You've got me on the go!
Fascinating Rhythm,
I'm all a-quiver.

What a mess you're making!
The neighbors want to know
Why I'm always shaking
Just like a flivver.

Each morning I get up with the sun—
Start a-hopping,
Never stopping—
To find at night no work has been done.

I know that
Once it didn't matter—
But now you're doing wrong;
When you start to patter
I'm so unhappy.

## Not for a Musicologist

Won't you take a day off?
Decide to run along
Somewhere far away off—
And make it snappy!

Oh, how I long to be the man I used to be!
Fascinating Rhythm,
Oh, won't you stop picking on me?

---

The following note is excerpted from Isaac Goldberg's *George Gershwin* (Simon and Schuster, 1931):

" 'When George was in London doing *Primrose,*' Ira relates, 'he wrote the first eight bars of what afterwards became Fascinating Rhythm. Alex Aarons, who was with him, and who is one of the keenest judges of a smart tune among the managers, told him to develop it for the next show. George didn't finish the tune until weeks later in New York. It was a tricky rhythm for those days, and it took me several days to decide on the rhyme scheme. I didn't think I had *the* brilliant title in Fascinating Rhythm but A, it *did* sing smoothly, and B,—I couldn't think of a better. The rhyme scheme was a, b, a, c,—a, b, a, c. When I got to the 8th line I showed the lyric to George. His comment was that the 4th and 8th lines should have a double (or two-syllable) rhyme where I had rhymed them with single syllables. I protested and, by singing, showed him that the last note in both lines had the same strength as the note preceding. To me the last two notes in these lines formed a spondee; the easiest way out was arbitrarily to put the accent on the last note. But this George couldn't see, and so, on and off, we argued for days. Finally I had to capitulate and write the lines as they are today:

4th line:     I'm all a-*quiv*er.
8th line:     —Just like a *fliv*ver,

after George proved to me that I had better use the double rhyme; because, whereas in singing, the notes might be considered even, in conducting the music, the downbeat came on the penultimate note.' "

\*     \*     \*

My father was not unmusical, but sometimes he couldn't recall the title of a song as clearly as he could the melody. To him this one frequently was "Fashion on the River."

✳   ✳   ✳

*"Finale Ultimo" Note.* In the Twenties it was almost *de rigueur* in the finale of a show to wind up the plot and relationships by setting new lyrics to one of the principal songs. For example: In *Lady, Be Good!* four couples, each formerly at odds, reunited at eleven p.m. each evening to "Fascinating Rhythm." After a cue such as "How about our getting hitched?" the first couple sang:

> Fascinating wedding,
> That sure appeals to me.
> Fascinating wedding,
> I hear you calling.

*Second pair:*

> Why not make it double?
> Please say that you agree.
> Saves a lot of trouble
> And sounds enthralling.

*Third set:*

> Now that misunderstanding is through,
> Aren't we silly
> Being chilly?
> What's to stop me from marrying you?

In the next eight bars the fourth couple decided they too would merge, and in the last eight the four suddenly engaged men, *unisono,* wound up with:

> Oh, what a busy day in church
> There's going to be.
> Fascinating wedding,
> You're calling my lady and me.

174

# HARLEM RIVER CHANTY *

TIP-TOES (1925). Music, George Gershwin. Opening, Act II.
Guests and Sailors aboard a yacht off Palm Beach, Florida.

When our supply of pieces of eight
   Is getting rather scanty,
And we are all unable to spend
   The night at penny ante,
'Tis then we burst into a refrain—
   *Allegro* and *andante*—
And sing that rollicking, frolicking strain,
   The Harlem River Chanty:

### 1

It's great to be a sailor,
   No life is quite so free;
     And the right boat
     Is the night boat
   Heading for Albany.

Yo-ho-ho, and a bottle of milk shake,
Yo-ho-ho, and a bottle of sass',
Yo-ho-ho, with a celery tonic—
Yo-ho-ho, fill up the glass!

### 2

Heave to! Me precious hearties!
   The sea life I adore.
     I've so much affection
     In that direction—
   I always hug the shore.

Yo-ho-ho, and a bottle of Bevo,
Yo-ho-ho, and a demi-tasse,
Yo-ho-ho, with a frosted coffee—
Yo-ho-ho, fill up the glass!

3

I've been aboard a whaler
And every sort of bark,
But there is no boat
Like a row boat
Out on Central Park.

Yo-ho-ho, and a pineapple phosphate,
Yo-ho-ho, and a bottle of sass',
Yo-ho-ho, with a choc'late malted—
Yo-ho-ho, fill up the glass!

---

Since the first four lines of the introduction were rendered slowly, and the last four in accelerated tempo, the line *"Allegro and andante"* should be, if ordered sense prevailed, *"Andante and allegro."* Obviously the reason for reversal is that *"andante"* was easier to rhyme.

\*     \*     \*

This tribute to soft drink (outside of Bevo, a beverage permitted to have a tiny alcoholic content) was an attempt at irony in a Prohibition Era when bathtub gin and flavored alcohol flooded the country, and pocket-flask manufacture was at its peak. (Personally, I prefer soft drinks, but of course had to have a bootlegger or else be a social pariah.)

I note that "sass' " (shortened from "sarsaparilla") makes two appearances to rhyme with "glass." This is unusual in that I ordinarily try not to use the same rhyme twice in a refrain. But I was stuck because even today I can dig up only a non-alcoholic, distasteful "Seltzer gas"; "Bass," an ale; and the Russian beer, *"kvass."*

176

# MISCHA, JASCHA, TOSCHA, SASCHA

Party song of the Twenties. Music, George Gershwin. *"A la humoresque."* Sung by the writers at the slightest provocation.

## 1

We really think you ought to know
   That we were born right in the middle
     Of Darkest Russia.
When we were three years old or so,
   We all began to play the fiddle
     In Darkest Russia.
      When we began,
    Our notes were sour—
      Until a man
     (Professor Auer)
Set out to show us, one and all,
How we could pack them in, in Carnegie Hall.

### Refrain

Temp'ramental Oriental Gentlemen are we:
   Mischa, Jascha, Toscha, Sascha—
     Fiddle-lee, diddle-lee, dee.
Shakespeare says, "What's in a name?"
     With him we disagree.
   Names like Sammy, Max or Moe
   Never bring the heavy dough
Like Mischa, Jascha, Toscha, Sascha—
     Fiddle-lee, diddle-lee, dee.

2

Though born in Russia, sure enough,
  We're glad that we became relations
    Of Uncle Sammy.
For though we play the high-brow stuff,
  We also like the syncopations
    Of Uncle Sammy.
      Our magic bow
    Plays Liszt and Schumann;
      But then you know
    We're only human
And like to shake a leg to jazz.
(Don't think we've not the feelings everyone has.)

*Refrain*

Temp'ramental Oriental Gentlemen are we:
  Mischa, Jascha, Toscha, Sascha—
    Fiddle-lee, diddle-lee, dee.
High-brow He-brow may play low-brow
  In his privacy.
  But when concert halls are packed,
  Watch us stiffen up and act
Like Mischa, Jascha, Toscha, Sascha—
  Fiddle-lee, diddle-lee, dee.

---

*Party Song.* I liked the sound—*circa* 1921—of the given names of four internationally renowned violinists then living in New York. As a consequence this song, written merely for our own amusement—no vehicle in mind.

Popular with musicians and instrumentalists at informal musicales, this opus surely must have been one of the best-known unpublished and non-commercial hits of the Twenties. Especially was it called for when any one of the four Russian-born—all American citizens now—was present: Mischa Elman, born in Talnoe; Jascha

Heifitz, Vilna; Toscha Seidel, Odessa; and Sascha Jacobsen, Finland—at that time part of Russia.

When Random House in 1932 was preparing a three-hundred-copy, signed, de luxe edition of *George Gershwin's Song-Book* (eighteen songs plus rather tricky piano transcriptions), they decided a novel item could be added to their twenty-dollar issue by a cover-insert of something as yet unpublished. And that's how a party song, "Mischa, &c.," which was really never intended to see print, achieved publication.

*     *     *

To show that there was no jealousy among top virtuosi regarding one another's artistry and drawing-power, this excerpt from an additional verse:

> We are the best—
> (The critics said it);
> But to the rest
> We still give credit.
> And so we want it understood
> We think that Paganini also was good.

*     *     *

*Violin Stand.* Shortly after my brother George began studying piano (when we were kids on Second Avenue) our younger brother Arthur started on violin. But it wasn't long before he quit. His principal complaint was that George, when taking a lesson, sat down—whereas he, taking one, had to stand up.

179

# THE REAL AMERICAN FOLK SONG
## *(Is a Rag)*

**LADIES FIRST (1918). Music, George Gershwin. *"Allegretto."***

> Near Barcelona the peasant croons
> The old traditional Spanish tunes;
> The Neapolitan Street Song sighs—
> You think of Italian skies.
> Each nation has a creative vein
> Originating a native strain,
> With folk songs plaintive and others gay
> In their own peculiar way.
> American folk songs, I feel,
> Have a much stronger appeal.

> *Refrain*
> The real American folk song is a rag—
> A mental jag—
> A rhythmic tonic for the chronic blues.
> The critics called it a joke song, but now
> They've changed their tune and they like it somehow.
> For it's inoculated
> With a syncopated
> Sort of meter,
> Sweeter
> Than a classic strain;
> Boy! You can't remain
> Still and quiet—
> For it's a riot!
> The real American folk song
> Is like a Fountain of Youth:
> You taste, and it elates you,
> And then invigorates you.
> The real American folk song—
> A master stroke song—
> IS A RAG!

## Not for a Musicologist

### Second Verse

You may dislike or you may adore
The native songs from a foreign shore;
They may be songs that you can't forget,
They may be distinctive, yet—
They lack a something: a certain snap,
The tempo ticklish that makes you tap,
The invitation to agitate—
And leave the rest to Fate.
A raggy refrain anytime
Sends me a message sublime.

---

*A Note of Minor Historicity.* This lyric is a late inclusion, because the song—

A. Was written in the spring of 1918.

B. Was liked by Nora Bayes, the star of *Ladies First.*

C. Was interpolated in that show in the fall of 1918.

D. Was my first lyric in any show.

E. Lasted eight or nine weeks. (New numbers were constantly being introduced by Miss Bayes, book show or not.)

F. Earned nothing. (Not that that mattered. I would gladly have paid for the honor, had I been asked—presupposing, of course, I were flush.)

G. Has lain low for over forty years.

H. Has recently been discussed in *The Gershwin Years* (by Edward Jablonski and Lawrence D. Stewart), arousing some faint interest on the part of a couple of recording companies. Whereupon, our music-publisher

I. Has seen fit to go to the expense of putting it out. So—

J. Some forty years after its inception the song is now available to the half-dozen or so collectors who might wish to buy a copy.

# SWEET AND LOW-DOWN

TIP-TOES (1925). Music, George Gershwin. "In a jazzy man-
ner." Sung, kazooed, tromboned, and danced by Andrew Tombes,
Lovey Lee, Gertrude McDonald, and Ensemble at a party, Palm
Beach.

There's a cabaret in *this* city
I can recommend to you;
Peps you up like electricity
When the band is blowing blue.
They play nothing classic, oh no! down there;
They crave nothing else but the low-down there.
If you need a tonic,
And the need is chronic—
If you're in a crisis,
My advice is:

*Refrain*

Grab a cab and go down
To where the band is playing;
Where milk and honey flow down;
Where ev'ry one is saying,
"Blow that Sweet and Low-Down!"

Busy as a beaver,
You'll dance until you totter;
You're sure to get the fever
For nothing could be hotter—
Oh, that Sweet and Low-Down!

Philosopher or deacon,
You simply have to weaken.
Hear those shuffling feet—
You can't keep your seat—
Professor, start your beat!

## Not for a Musicologist

Come along, get in it—
You'll love the syncopation!
The minute they begin it,
You're shouting to the nation:
 "Blow that Sweet and Low-Down!"

---

Before Ukulele Ike in *Lady, Be Good!* accepted our "Little Jazz Bird" for his specialty spot, he had rejected something we'd concocted called "Singin' Pete"—"the reason for shufflin' feet." (We didn't particularly fancy "Singin' Pete" but thought Ike would.) A year later I remembered from this discarded attempt at something patently popular one line I liked: "He's the John McCormack of the sweet and low-down." So I salvaged for a title the portmanteau phrase, arrived at from "sweet and low" and "low-down."

\*　　\*　　\*

It makes for small philological honor, but one is pleased to note that invented phrases like "sweet and low-down" and *Of Thee I Sing*'s "with a hey, nonny nonny and a ha cha cha!" are included in *The American Thesaurus of Slang*.

As for "portmanteau" in its application to words and phrases rather than luggage, credit Lewis Carroll. In *Through the Looking Glass,* Humpty-Dumpty explains to Alice the meaning of some of the words in "Jabberwocky." After "brillig," he analyzes "slithy": "Well, *slithy* means 'lithe and slimy.' You see it's like a portmanteau—there are two meanings packed in one word."

(Re this contraction device—in *The American Language: Supplement One,* Mencken evidences a preference for "blends" to "portmanteau-words." And others, since Carroll, prefer other coinages, such as "telescope-words," "amalgams," &c. But enough of Carrollinguistics.)

# THAT LOST BARBER SHOP CHORD

AMERICANA (1926). Music, George Gershwin. "Pseudo-spiritually." Harlem barber shop setting. Sung by Louis Lazarin and the Pan-American Quartet.

Seated one day at the barber's,
A place up in Harlem that harbors
Four barbers who certainly could harmonize,
I listened to them in amazement—
Not caring what minutes or days meant—
For Lordy! they certainly could vocalize.
Suddenly I heard them strike a chord,
Felt my miseries go overboard,
Seemed as if I heard the angels hum,
Seemed as if I were in Kingdom Come.
"Oh, sing it again!" I entreated,
But oh! it was never repeated.
I cried out and cried out, . . .
But it died out.

### Refrain

I'm looking for that lost barber shop chord—
Where can it be?
I'm looking for that lost barber shop chord—
Come back to me!
I'm growing gray,
Searching nighttime and day;
When is it coming to stay?
I'm looking for that lost barber shop chord—
Sweet misery!—
For it will bring eternal jubilee.
I'm looking high,
I'm looking low,
Before I die
I want to know
What happened to that heav'nly lost barber shop chord.
Where can it be, where can it,
WHERE CAN IT BE?

## Not for a Musicologist

This, like "Sweet and Low-Down," has a portmanteau title. The derivation is of course from "The Lost Chord," Sullivan's setting of the Adelaide Proctor poem, and "Play That Barber Shop Chord," by MacDonald, Tracey, and Muir. (Incid., checking in the anthologies, I find that the Proctor poem is called "A Lost Chord." Whoever—Sir Arthur?—changed the indefinite to the definite article in the title did the song no harm. An 1893 quote: " 'The Lost Chord,' perhaps the most successful song of modern times. . . ." (Willeby: *Masters of English Music.*) And a 1928 quote: "It has been computed that 'The Lost Chord' is one of the six most popular songs ever written." (Isaac Goldberg: *The Story of Gilbert and Sullivan.*) Sorry, Goldberg doesn't state all the five others, only two: Nevin's "The Rosary" and Faure's *"Les Rameaux."* As for the 1910 "Play That Barber Shop Chord"—it isn't one of The Six, but it certainly is one of the best ragtime songs ever written.)

Our song, "That Lost Barber Shop Chord," got lost pronto 11:15 p.m. closing night of *Americana,* and remains to this day a six-page sheet-music nonentity. But it had its day—one or two days anyway. The critics more than liked it. Here's how Charles Pike Sawyer in the *New York Evening Post* reviewed it, 7/27/26: "that wonderfully beautiful 'Lost Barber Shop Chord' . . . is Gershwin at his best, which is saying a lot. Full of beautiful melody and swinging rhythm, it was a perfect joy, and right well was it sung by Louis Lazarin and a Negro quartet with delightful voices." And on 7/31/26 he insisted: "What a joy is George Gershwin's 'Lost Barber Shop Chord' . . . and fully the equal of anything this great American composer has written, even in that gloriously beautiful tone poem—he called it a piano concerto, which it wasn't —played last season by Walter Damrosch's New York Symphony Orchestra." Stephen Rathbun, *New York Evening Sun,* 7/27/26: "The music of the revue is quite as attractive as the humor. The high mark is George Gershwin's ambitious 'Lost Barber Shop Chord.' " And Others.

Possibly these judgments were to some degree correct at the time. Me, I haven't heard the song sung anywhere in over thirty years.

# TSCHAIKOWSKY
## (and Other Russians)

LADY IN THE DARK (1941). Music, Kurt Weill. *"Allegro barbaro."* Refrain of forty-nine Russian composers rattled off in thirty-nine seconds by Danny Kaye.

> Without the least excuse
> Or the slightest provocation,
> May I fondly introduce,
> For your mental delectation,
> The names that always give me brain concussion,
> The names of those composers known as Russian.

### Refrain

There's Malichevsky, Rubinstein, Arensky and Tschaikowsky,
Sapelnikoff, Dimitrieff, Tscherepnin, Kryjanowsky,
Godowsky, Arteiboucheff, Moniuszko, Akimenko,
Solovieff, Prokofieff, Tiomkin, Korestchenko.
There's Glinka, Winkler, Bortniansky, Rebikoff, Ilyinsky,
There's Medtner, Balakireff, Zolotareff and Kvoschinsky.
And Sokoloff and Kopyloff, Dukelsky and Klenowsky,
And Shostakovitsch, Borodine, Gliere and Nowakofski.
There's Liadoff and Karganoff, Markievitch, Pantschenko
And Dargomyzski, Stcherbatcheff, Scriabine, Vassilenko,
Stravinsky, Rimsky-Korsakoff, Mussorgsky and Gretchaninoff
And Glazounoff and Caesar Cui, Kalinikoff, Rachmaninoff,
> Stravinsky and Gretchaninoff,
> Rumshinsky and Rachmaninoff,
I really have to stop, the subject has been dwelt upon enough!

### Ensemble

He'd *better* stop because we feel we all have undergone enough!

## Not for a Musicologist

This lyric, proper noun for proper noun, is based almost entirely on a bit of light verse called "The Music Hour," by Arthur Francis, in the then pre-pictorial, humorous weekly *Life,* June 12, 1924; and for which Mr. Francis received a check of twelve dollars from the editors. I have waited hopefully—but in vain—these many years for someone to accuse me of plagiarism, so that I could respond with the fact that for four years or so I was the pseudonymous Arthur Francis (cf. note below). The names of most of the forty-nine composers mentioned I compiled from advertisements on the back covers of piano music and orchestral scores in my brother's collection.

*　　*　　*

Not all of the forty-nine, however, have been necessarily merely names to me. *Rumshinsky,* who wrote many musical-comedy scores for the Yiddish theater, I met several times when I lived on Second Avenue in New York; he was a pinochle-playing companion of my father's. Dimitri *Tiomkin,* now one of the topflight Hollywood film composers (rich also in the possession of one of the topmost Russian accents extant), I have known since the Twenties. With ballet and oratorio composer *Dukelsky,* whom I first knew as Vladimir Dukelsky, later as Vernon Duke (a name suggested to him by my brother), I collaborated on the *Ziegfeld Follies of 1936.* And through Vernon I met both *Stravinsky* (at the Met, 1935, during intermission of *Lady Macbeth of Mtsensk*) and *Prokofieff* (at my publisher's, New York, 1938. He was on his way back to Russia from Hollywood and I got him a copy of *Porgy and Bess,* which he wanted to take along). *Godowsky* I'd met in Paris on several occasions—this two years before his son Leo, musician and inventor, married my sister. And in January 1956, during a two-week stay in Moscow (I flew there for the opening of *Porgy and Bess*) I met Reinhold Moritzovich *Glière,* composer of "The Red Poppy" and some five hundred other works. This was at a luncheon given by the cultural organization called VOKS. At another table my wife, through an interpreter, told the affable and charming octogenarian that I had mentioned him in a song about Russian composers. Afterwards I was introduced to Glière and was somewhat embarrassed by his profuse thanks, since he didn't know there were forty-eight other mentions —all put together for comedic effect of names generally strange to American ears. I never met *Rachmaninoff*—but my brother knew him quite well. Rachmaninoff? I really have to stop—the subject has been dwelt upon enough.

\*    \*    \*

*New World Record.* In the legend beneath the title, I state that Danny Kaye rattled off "Tschaikowsky" in thirty-nine seconds. However, during a world-wide tour for the UN International Children's Emergency Fund he announced on the stage in Barcelona he would try for a world record in the delivery of this song—and was timed in thirty-six seconds. But this went by the wayside when in Madrid he was clocked in thirty-one.

\*    \*    \*

*Pseudonym.* Early in 1920 in Chicago there was a successful show called *The Sweetheart Shop.* One day, some weeks before this musical was to make its New York debut, George learned that its management wanted a new song for ingénue Helen Ford. So, hopefully, that night, in a period when the musical-comedy cycle called for at least one Pollyanna song in a show, we wrote something called "Waiting for the Sun to Come Out."

Next day George got in touch with producer Edgar MacGregor, who was in New York and was willing to listen. For fear that if MacGregor learned the song was a sibling collaboration he might listen to it skeptically, I suggested that the lyricist be called Arthur Francis—a combination of the prenames of our younger brother, Arthur, and our sister, Frances. MacGregor liked the song, then asked: "Who's Arthur Francis?" "Oh, he's a clever college boy with lots of talent," said George (as he later told me). The asking price of $250 for the song was agreeable to MacGregor. A couple of weeks later the song went in, was rehearsed, and was mentioned in all the reviews.

The acclaim given the show in the Loop—it ran three months there—wasn't repeated on Broadway. During its third week in New York, when MacGregor was reminded of the as yet unpaid $250, he confided that business was very bad and it looked as though the show would close in two or three weeks. "I'm working, so I don't mind not being paid myself if things are that tough," said George, "but the college boy really needs the money." Whereupon a most welcome check for $125 was made out to Arthur Francis. "Waiting for the Sun" was my first published song. The $125, plus, within the year, earnings of $723.40 from sheet music and $445.02 from phonograph records, kept the "college boy" going for some time.

(As Arthur Francis I did the lyrics for *Two Little Girls in Blue,* with composers Youmans and Lannin; *A Dangerous Maid,* with my brother; and a dozen or so songs interpolated in various revues, with composers Lewis Gensler, Raymond Hubbell, Milton Schwarzwald, and one or two others. In 1924 I dropped Arthur Francis. He was beginning to be confused with lyricist Arthur Jackson; also I'd been made aware that there was an English lyricist named Arthur Francis. Besides, all who knew me knew me as a Gershwin anyway.)

# A Set of Sagas

*"The Ballad of Baby Face McGinty"*

*"The Jolly Tar and the Milkmaid"*

*"The Princess of Pure Delight"*

*"Sam and Delilah"*

*"The Saga of Jenny"*

# THE BALLAD OF
# BABY FACE MCGINTY
## (Who Bit Off More Than He Could Chew)

ZIEGFELD FOLLIES OF 1936. Music, Vernon Duke. Sung by
Judy Canova, as Maw, to her three bearded sons in a Kentucky
cabin. (Omitted here are the vocal repeats by the sons.) The
lights dim down after each stanza, blacking out the cabin interior,
and come up on the ballet action of gangsters and T-Men.

1

Oh, Baby Face McGinty—
His story I will tell.
At seven his heart was flinty,
Though he looked as cute as hell.
He stole his granny's false teeth
To buy himself some gin.
The games of the other kids he'd shelve;
He was a pappy when he was.twelve.
Oh, Baby Face McGinty
Was not what he might 'a' been.

2

McGinty ruled St. Louie
When he was twenty-one.
To see the police go screwy
Was Baby's idee of fun.
Each day he'd hold a bank up;
He dealt in booze—and how!
Machine guns he owned filled forty trucks,
And he had hidden three million bucks.
Said Baby Face McGinty,
"Oh, I'm goin' places now!"

### 3

He won new territory
Each hour of the day.
Soon Baby was in his glory;
Ten gov'nors were in his pay.
He killed, he raped, he arsoned—
But never did he swing.
He put Jesse James right on the shelf;
The devil, he acted like God Hisself.
Was none but feared McGinty,
And no one could do a thing.

### 4

"Get Baby Face McGinty!"
Said Mr. Morgenthau.
"He cheated on taxes, di'n't he?
That's one thing we can't allow!"
They got, they shot McGinty;
They never gave a damn.
For you're up against true ma-ni-acs,
When you don't pay up your income tax.
The moral of McGinty
Is: Don't cheat your Uncle Sam.

(*The lights go up on all participating as they wave American flags and sing:*)

So long, good-bye, McGinty—
On one thing you were lax:
You could get away with murder,
But not on your income tax.

---

*R.I.P. "B. F. McGinty."* During the tryout of the *Follies* in Boston this combination hillbilly-gangster-T-Man song-ballet was staged one night; and as choreographed by Balanchine and costumed by Minnelli, I thought it a stunner. And so did many others. But this *Follies* was rare in that although the customary out-of-town phrase "It needs work" applied, the problem here was one of wealth of material rather than lack. With a cast containing, among others, Fanny Brice, Bob Hope, Eve Arden, and Judy Canova, there was a more than usual amount of comedy; there were plenty of stageable songs and special material (because of production postponements Duke and I had been at it eight or nine months, and twenty-five numbers were available); there was high-spirited dancing directed by Robert Alton; and there were ballets by Balanchine: "5 a.m." for Josephine Baker, "Night Flight" for ballerina Harriet Hoctor, "Words without Music" ("A Surrealist Ballet"), and "McGinty."

In his autobiography, *Passport to Paris,* Vernon writes: "A fresh and novel 'Ballad of Baby Face McGinty,' imaginatively staged by Balanchine, was inexplicably dropped in Boston." Inexplicable, yes—if ousting depended on quality alone. But we had too much show with too many elaborate production numbers, and "McGinty" was one of the discarded.

The business of stage entertainment is precarious enough without the producer's having to worry about such matters as stagehands' extra pay and Suburbia's railroad schedules. So, unless you are Richard Wagner or Eugene O'Neill, overlength has to be considered. The Show Must Go On—but not too long after eleven p.m.

# THE JOLLY TAR AND THE MILKMAID

A DAMSEL IN DISTRESS (1937). Music, George Gershwin. *"Allegretto scherzando."* Sung in Totleigh Castle by the Belpher Society for the Preservation of Traditional English Ballads, Madrigals, and Rounds.

### 1

There was a jolly British tar
  Who met a milkmaid bonny.
He said, "How beautiful you are."
  With a hey and a nonny,
  With a hey and a nonny.
"Such golden hair I ne'er did see,
  With lips to shame the cherry—
Oh, buxom milkmaid, marry me!"
  With a down-a-derry,
  With a down-a, down-a-derry.

### *Refrain*

"Our hearts could rhyme," said she.
" 'Tis flattered I'm;" said she,
    "But oh, ah me,
    You see, you see,
    You see, you see
    I happen to be,
    I happen to be
    The mother of three,
    A wife already
    And mother of three,
Of three, of three, of three, of three, of three—
    The mother of three!"

2

The jolly tar, he laughed a laugh.
" 'Tis for the best, my bonny,
That you won't be my better half."
    With a hey and a nonny,
    With a hey and a nonny.
"I near forgot on seeing you
    That I've a wife in Kerry,
In Spain and also Timbuktu."
    With a down-a-derry,
    With a down-a, down-a-derry.

*Refrain*

"You've got me thinkin' twice;
Good-bye to shoes and rice,
        For oh, ah me,
        Just now, you see,
        Just now, you see
        I happen to be,
        I happen to be
        The husband of three,
        A-spliced already
        And husband of three,
Of three, of three, of three, of three, of three—
        The husband of three!"

---

*"Without Appreciable Meaning."* The introduction of a group of madrigal singers in *Damsel in Distress* permitted the writing of a couple of pieces in the style, and with the flavor, of several centuries ago. In "The Jolly Tar and the Milkmaid" we tried for the feel of an English eighteenth-century light ballad. The "With a hey and a nonny" and "With a down-a, down-a-derry" inclusions, though, are refrain phrases ordinarily associated with songs of an earlier period. These and similar sixteenth-century phrases were attached to the stanzas of many songs for jingle quality and sing-

ability. They made little or no sense otherwise. For, according to *The Oxford English Dictionary,* "derry" (the year 1553 its first appearance in print) was "a meaningless word in the refrains of popular songs"; "down," as an adverb (1598), "used in ballad refrains without appreciable meaning"; and "nonny-nonny" (1533) "a meaningless refrain often used to cover indelicate allusions."

The other piece we did was a short contrapuntal exercise originally called "Back to Bach" and here newly worded to "Sing of Spring." It contained imagined refrain lines like "Sing willy-wally-willo," "Sing tilly-tally-tillo," "Piminy mo," and "Tra la la lo."

$$* \quad * \quad *$$

*Additional Uttered Nonsense.* I have just spent the afternoon leafing through the thousand or so songs in D'Urfey's six-volume collection, *Pills to Purge Melancholy* (published 1719–20), to see how frequently various meaningless but singable phrases occurred in that period. Well, most of the songs use the short refrain, but most of these are meaningful (far too much so—unless one is an Erotica buff). Fixing upon only the innocuous, I find that the Elizabethan "hey nonny" and such were by then on the wane. The most favored refrain in the collection—some twenty songs use it—seems to have been "with a fa la la . . ." (incid., "fal la la" was a favorite refrain with Gilbert and Sullivan). Other of the innocent burthens in D'Urfey are: "with a hey ding, hoe ding, derry, derry, ding," "with a fadariddle la . . . ," "fa la la, lanky downdilly," "hey troly loly lo," and "with a humbledum grumbledum hey." Not forgetting an exuberant "huggle duggle, ha! ha! ha!"

The use of the easily assimilable nonsense phrase in song is of course not limited to the British, Irish, and Scottish. Hundreds of examples can be found in nineteenth- and twentieth-century American song. Offhand: "doodah, doodah," "yip i addy i ay," "ja da, ja da, jing, jing, jing," all the variants of "ho de ho" and "hi de hi," &c., &c. These are not necessarily all used as refrains—they may be titles, interjections, responses, or whatever. A longish example of the phrase-for-sound-alone's-sake is "It Ain't Neces-

sarily So" 's "Wadoo! Zim bam boddle-oo! Hoodle ah da wah da!
Scatty wah!"

*     *     *

Dramatist Thomas D'Urfey (1653–1723) included a number of
his own songs in *Pills to Purge Melancholy*. And I cannot take
leave of the collection without quoting the charmingly informative
heading to one of them: "Advice to the City, a famous Song, set
to a tune of Signior Opdar, so remarkable, that I had the Honour
to Sing it with King Charles at Windsor; He holding one part of
the Paper with Me."

# THE PRINCESS OF PURE DELIGHT

LADY IN THE DARK (1941). Music, Kurt Weill. *"Andantino grazioso."* Gertrude Lawrence as Liza Elliott to a group of children, during the Second Dream Sequence.

The Prince in Orange and the Prince in Blue,
And the Prince whose raiment was of Lavender hue—
They sighed and they suffered and they tossed at night
For the neighboring Princess of Pure Delight. . . .
   (Who was secretly in love with a Minstrel)

Her father, the King, didn't know which to choose;
There were two charming suitors he'd have to refuse.
So he called for the Dean of his Sorcerers and
Inquired which one was to win her hand.
   (Which they always did in those days)

"My King, here's a riddle—(you test them tonight):
'What word of five letters is never spelled right?
What word of five letters is always spelled wrong?'
The one who can answer will be wedded ere long.
   That will be twenty gulden, please."

The King called the three and he told them the test,
The while his fair daughter kept beating her breast.
He put them the riddle. They failed (as he feared).
Then all of a sudden the Minstrel appeared!
   (Quite out of breath)

"I'll answer that riddle," cried the Singer of Song.
"What's never spelled 'right' in five letters is 'wrong,'
And it's right to spell 'wrong'—w-r-o-n-g!
Your Highness, the Princess belongeth to me.
   And I love her, anyway!"

A Set of Sagas

"Be off with you, villain!" the King cried in rage,
"For my Princess a Prince—not a man from the stage."
"But, Sire!" said the Minstrel, " 'tis love makes me say
No King who's a real King treats lovers this way!
    It isn't sporting.

And if you're no real King, no Princess is she—
And if she's no Princess then she can wed me!"
"By gad," cried His Highness, "you handsome young knave,
I fear me you're right!" and his blessing he gave,
    As a trumpeter began to trumpet.

The Princess then quickly came out of her swoon
And she looked at her swain and her world was in tune.
And the castle soon rang with cheer and with laughter.
(And of course they lived happily ever after)

---

*Fairy Tale from Left Field.* During the writing of *Lady in the Dark* Kurt Weill and I spent a couple of weekends with Moss Hart at his charming summer place in Bucks County. The food was excellent, the guestrooms cozy; there were a large swimming pool and thousands of trees and any amount of huge and overwhelmingly friendly, woolly dogs; there was even that rarity for those days (1940), a TV set; but the show was ever on our minds and mostly we were at it, discussing the score in progress and what lay ahead. Dinner, though, usually brought additional guests; and one Sunday night Richard Rodgers, who had been weekending at nearby George Kaufman's, offered us a ride back to the city (we had come by train), a convenience gladly accepted. We were to leave about nine p.m., but it was decided to wait until city-bound traffic died down a bit. To pass the time, Dick picked an old quiz-and-conundrum book of the Twenties from Moss's shelves; and all present spent an hour or so answering quiz questions, correcting twisted quotations, solving riddles, &c. End of Part One.

Some weeks later when Kurt and I were on the Second Dream Sequence we came to a spot where Liza and some children were alone on the stage. I suggested—and Kurt liked the notion—that here a sung fairy tale might be incorporated. So next day I got hold of some Andersen and the Brothers Grimm, and leafed through for something not too well known to base a narrative on —any short one that could be transformed into a song. In my anxiousness to find something quickly, probably much possible was overlooked; my hurried impressions pictured mainly young princes turning into frogs and vice versa. Which form of corporeal alchemy seemed too complicated and farfetched. Metamorphosis out, I began thinking of other legendary magical gimmicks and concluded that the kind used so frequently in *The Arabian Nights' Entertainments* might do the trick: one where an in-a-spot young man answers brilliantly one or several loaded questions, and reaps, from an amazed and delighted potentate, rewards of non-decapitation, bushels of diamonds and rubies, a harem, and other desiderata. It was then that I remembered the Sunday night mentioned above and *my* brilliant answer to a conundrum Dick put: "What word of five letters is never spelled right?" This seemed short, sweet, and possible for a device; so, having something to head for, I started.

I had a rough idea of what I wanted to say, but none about the number of lines it would take. I finally decided on a title and came up with an opening stanza, which I gave to Kurt for tentative setting. Tentative because I was prepared to change the approach if he felt that a longish lyric with regular, confining stanzas might make for musical monotony. Soon after, he played me a setting I liked; then said there'd be no problem—that, no matter how many stanzas were required, the musical end would be reasonably cohesive. With this assurance I kept furthering and tickling up the narrative, with Kurt never more than a stanza behind me; and in a few days this section of the dream was completed.

$$* \quad * \quad *$$

Because several of my friends were being analyzed at twenty dollars a session, I couldn't resist "That will be twenty gulden, please."

# SAM AND DELILAH

GIRL CRAZY (1930). Music, George Gershwin. *"Tempo di Blues."* Ethel Merman as Frisco Kate, in a Western saloon.

Delilah was a floozy;
She never gave a damn.
Delilah wasn't choosy
    Till she fell
    For a swell
Buckaroo whose name was Sam.

Delilah got in action;
Delilah did her kootch.
She gave him satisfaction
    And he fell
    'Neath her spell
With the aid of love and hooch.

But one day—so they tell us—
His true wife he did crave.
Delilah, she got jealous
    And she tracked him
    And hacked him
And dug for Sam a grave.

It's always that way with passion,
    So, cowboy, learn to behave,
Or else you're li'ble to cash in
    With no tombstone on your grave.

Delilah, oh, Delilah!
She's no babe in the wood;
Run, cowboy, run a mile-ah!
    If you love
    That kind of
Woman she'll do you no good!

\*     \*     \*

The Sheriff got Delilah.
They swung her from a tree.
The records are on file-ah.
It's distressin'—
But the lesson
Is an easy one to see.

---

Acceptable pronunciation (and exigency) permit "passion" to rhyme with "cash in"; and "distressin' " with "lesson." What wasn't good lyric-writing, I see now, is the placing of "hooch" and "kootch" on long, full notes of a slow-blues tune. These words should be uttered quickly so that the listener hears them as monosyllables; not duo, as "hoo–ch" and "koo–tch." I got away with it, thanks to Merman's ability to sustain any note any human or humane length of time. Few singers could give you *koo* for seven beats (it runs into the next bar, like intermission people) and come through with a terrifically convincing *tch* at the end.

*Brief Glossary for the Very Young:* "Hooch" and "kootch" both entered our language in the 1890's. "Hooch" was a synonym for whisky in the Klondike, probably based on an intoxicating liquor developed earlier by the Hoochinoo Indians of Alaska; "kootch" from "hootchy-kootchy," a daring Oriental belly-dance viewed by the less respectable at the Chicago's World's Fair in 1893.

# THE SAGA OF JENNY

LADY IN THE DARK (1941). Music, Kurt Weill. *"Allegretto quasi andantino"*—actually, a sort of blues bordello. In the Third Dream Sequence, Gertrude Lawrence as Liza Elliott is being Tried for Breach of Promise. Having led Kendall Nesbitt to believe that she will marry him, she now Cannot Make Up Her Mind. Her Defense is that Dire Complications Frequently Result from Being Too Positive—as follows:

### Liza

There once was a girl named Jenny
Whose virtues were varied and many—
Excepting that she was inclined
Always to make up her mind;
And Jenny points a moral
With which you cannot quarrel—
    As you will find.

### Refrain

Jenny made her mind up when she was three
She, herself, was going to trim the Christmas tree.
Christmas Eve she lit the candles—tossed the taper away.
Little Jenny was an orphan on Christmas Day.

    Poor Jenny! Bright as a penny!
    Her equal would be hard to find.
      She lost one dad and mother,
      A sister and a brother—
      But she would make up her mind.

Jenny made her mind up when she was twelve
That into foreign languages she would delve;
But at seventeen to Vassar it was quite a blow
That in twenty-seven languages she couldn't say no.

Jenny made her mind up at twenty-two
To get herself a husband was the thing to do.
She got herself all dolled up in her satins and furs
And she got herself a husband—but he wasn't hers.

Jenny made her mind up at thirty-nine
She would take a trip to the Argentine.
She was only on vacation but the Latins agree
Jenny was the one who started the Good Neighbor Policy.

### Jury

Poor Jenny! Bright as a penny!
Her equal would be hard to find.
   Oh, passion doesn't vanish
   In Portuguese or Spanish—
But she would make up her mind.

### Liza

Jenny made her mind up at fifty-one
She would write her memoirs before she was done.
The very day her book was published, hist'ry relates
There were wives who shot their husbands in some
   thirty-three states.

### Jury

Poor Jenny! Bright as a penny!
Her equal would be hard to find.
   She could give cards and spade-ies
   To many other ladies—
But she would make up her mind.

### Liza

Jenny made her mind up at seventy-five
She would live to be the oldest woman alive.
But gin and rum and destiny play funny tricks,
And poor Jenny kicked the bucket at seventy-six.

## A Set of Sagas

### Jury

Jenny points a moral
With which we cannot quarrel.
Makes a lot of common sense!

### Liza

Jenny and her saga
Prove that you are gaga
If you don't keep sitting on the fence.

### Jury

Jenny and her story
Point the way to glory
To all man and womankind.

### All

Anyone with vision
Comes to this decision:
Don't make up—You shouldn't make up—
You mustn't make up—Oh, never make up—
Anyone with vision
Comes to this decision:
DON'T MAKE UP YOUR MIND!

---

The third musical dream sequence in *Lady in the Dark,* a mixture of Court Trial and Minstrel Show, was practically completed when it was decided that minstrel costume and background weren't novel enough. Agreeing that a circus setting seemed preferable—there could be more riotous color and regalia—we changed the opening, the jury patters, and most of the recitatives, from an environment of burnt cork and sanded floor to putty nose and tanbark.

One section of this sequence, however, remained unchanged: Liza Elliott's defense of her actions. It was a six- or seven-minute pseudo-metaphysical dissertation based on the signs of the Zodiac and their influences, all pretty fatalistic; in short, she'd done what she did because she couldn't help doing whatever she did do. We were quite proud of this bizarre and *Three Penny Opera*-like effort and felt it could be the play's musical highlight. (We wrote a fourth dream sequence, but this one was not for her analyst. It was a rather extravagant daydream—following a marriage proposal by the Western movie star—in which Liza envisions her possible Hollywood life: an enormous ranch in the San Fernando Valley with a palatial home furnished from the Hearst Collection, butlers galore, private golf course, Chinese cooks, fifty-thousand-barrel gushers on the property, &c. But this twenty-minute daydream—not to be heard by the analyst—was also unheard and unseen by the audience, as the show was already about fifteen or more minutes too long.) Anyway, after some four months of hard work—twelve to sixteen hours a day, and through one of the hottest summers New York had ever known—our contributions to *Lady in the Dark* were completed; and Kurt could now remain in New City across the Hudson to orchestrate, and I return home until the start of rehearsals.

I had been back in California only about a week when producer Sam Harris telephoned me. After long and careful consideration he and Moss Hart felt that the Zodiac number, impressive as it was, might prove too dour and oppressive; something lighter and perhaps gayer was required. I telephoned Kurt. His feeling was, right or wrong, we owed them a go at it, since, generally, everything else we'd done had been found so acceptable. So, a few days later I was again in New York. At one conference Moss had a suggestion that we do a number about a woman who couldn't make up her mind. That sounded possible; and after a week or so of experimenting with style, format, and complete change of melodic mood from the Zodiac song, we started "Jenny," and finished Liza's new defense about ten days later.

*    *    *

All through rehearsals Miss Lawrence did "Jenny" most acceptably. But I kept wondering whether it would be as effective as the

Zodiac song. This is what happened opening night in Boston: We were playing to a packed house, and the show was holding the audience tensely. It was working out. I was among the standees at the back of the house; next to me was one of the Sam Harris staff. In the circus scene when Danny Kaye completed the last note of "Tschaikowsky," thunderous applause rocked the theater for at least a solid minute. The staff member clutched my arm, muttered: "Christ, we've lost our star!," couldn't take it, and rushed for the lobby. Obviously he felt that nothing could top Danny's rendition, that "Jenny" couldn't compete with it, and that either Miss Lawrence would leave the show or that Danny Kaye would have to be cut down to size.

But he should have waited. The next few lines of dialogue weren't heard because of the continuing applause. Then, as Danny deferred to Miss Lawrence, it ended; and "Jenny" began. She hadn't been singing more than a few lines when I realized an interpretation we'd never seen at rehearsal was materializing. Not only were there new nuances and approaches, but on top of this she "bumped" it and "ground" it, to the complete devastation of the audience. At the conclusion, there was an ovation which lasted twice as long as that for "Tschaikowsky." "Tschaikowsky" had shown us the emergence of a new star in Danny Kaye. But "Jenny" revealed to us that we didn't have to worry about losing our brighter-than-ever star.

\*    \*    \*

It is easier to predict correctly what will happen to the stock market than what show numbers will do. One hopes for the best, but one best remains noncommittal. Not everyone does, though. Three or four nights after the Boston opening, with *Lady* looking like a big hit, Kurt told me he hadn't wanted to worry me but this is what occurred after the dress rehearsal. Hassard Short, a top revue man of excellent taste, in charge of the show's physical production and lighting, took Kurt aside and said: "If you'll take my advice, you boys had better get two new numbers ready in a hurry. You'll find that 'Jenny' and the Russian number won't make it."

# A Gathering of Guidance

*"Clap Yo' Hands"*

*"Lose That Long Face"*

*"One Life to Live"*

*"Slap That Bass"*

*"Strike Up the Band"*

# CLAP YO' HANDS

OH, KAY! (1926). Music, George Gershwin. "Spirited, but sustained." Exclaimed and stomped by Harlan Dixon and Ensemble in a Long Island drawing room.

> Come on, you children, gather around—
> > Gather around, you children.
> And we will lose that evil spirit
> > Called the Voodoo.

> Nothin' but trouble, if he has found,
> > If he has found you, children—
> But you can chase the Hoodoo
> With the dance that you do.

> > Let me lead the way.
> > Jubilee today! Say!
> > He'll never hound you;
> > Stamp on the ground, you children!

### *Refrain*

> Clap-a yo' hand! Slap-a yo' thigh!
> > Halleluyah! Halleluyah!
> Ev'rybody come along and join the Jubilee!

> Clap-a yo' hand! Slap-a yo' thigh!
> Don't you lose time! Don't you lose time!
> Come along—it's Shake Yo' Shoes Time
> > Now for you and me!

On the sands of time
You are only a pebble;
Remember, trouble must be treated
Just like a rebel;
Send him to the Debble!

Clap-a yo' hand! Slap-a yo' thigh!
Halleluyah! Halleluyah!
Ev'rybody come along and join the Jubilee!

---

*Two Matters: The First, Unimportant; The Second, Longer.*

1. Looking over some old worksheets, I notice that the original
and logical title for this song was "Clap-a Yo' Hand," a phrase
occurring three times in the refrain. Today, thirty-three years later
—sue me, third-degree me—I've no idea why I thought a better
title for sheet-music publication was "Clap Yo' Hands," a phrase
which doesn't appear in the song at all.

2. In "Clap Yo' Hands" the words of the refrain's first section
are repeated in the last. There is no attempt to wind up the lyric
with a verbal twist or variation. That's because "Clap Yo' Hands"
is basically a stage tune for dancing, vocally carrying a one-minded
invitation to Join the Jubilee. So the better part of lyric valor was to
avoid any verbal change which might impede the song's exhorta-
tory momentum before the dance.

Usually, though, when possible, a verbal twist or turn is striven
for. A simple one, for example, is an ending of "But Not for Me":

When ev'ry happy plot
Ends with the marriage knot—
And there's no knot for me.

Somewhat more elaborate is the wind-up of "Let's Call the Whole
Thing Off," when the disagreeing pair decide that separation might
be too great a dose of sweet sorrow, and switch to: "Better call the
calling-off off, /Let's call the *whole* thing off."

## A Gathering of Guidance

What I have just been vaguely informative about is, shall we say, a minor form of the trick or surprise ending, a structural device I have always liked. When I was very young I admired O. Henry, then later, Maupassant (as in "The Necklace"), and others like Bierce and John Collier. Also, in my late teens I fooled around with French verse forms, such as the triolet, villanelle, and especially the rondeau—with its opening phrase taking on new meanings when repeated. I even sold one to the New York *Sun*, for which I received three dollars:

### RONDEAU TO ROSIE

My Rosie knows the places where
One goes to lose all trace of care.
   The ultra swagger cabaret . . .
   The crystal chandeliered café . . .

And oh, she knows the waiters there.
Her wink will fetch from magic lair
A bottle of a vintage rare . . .
   And potent beer? Hot dog! I'll say
     My Rosie knows!

Without my Rosie, I declare
I'd plumb the depths of dark despair.
   To her I dedicate this lay;
   To her I owe my spirits gay,
   My smiling mien, my cheerful air,
     My rosy nose.

Whether it was worth three dollars or not, Buddy De Sylva liked it and thought it was an idea for us to collaborate on for a song lyric. But we never got around to it. Probably just as well.

\*　　\*　　\*

(*Special Note for Those Who Wonder Why Rosie Had to Wink:* Prohibition was in effect.)

215

# LOSE THAT LONG FACE

A STAR IS BORN (1954). Music, Harold Arlen. "Lightly" and "With a sweep." Judy Garland as an irrepressibly cheerful little newsboy, unstoppably bent on making euphoric those in the scene and in the audience.

Does the day look painful,
        The future glum?
Does the sky look rainful?
        Hey, there! Say, there:
        Are you in a vacuum?
All that stuff and nonsense
        You can overcome.
A long face gets you nowhere—
        You lose that Month of May.
Like Peter Pan, the sweeter pan
        Wins the day.

*Refrain*

Go lose that long face, that long face—
Go 'long and get that long face lost.
The blues black out when they can see
A smile that says, "Move on. No vacancy!"
        This panacea idea
I'm handing you without any cost.
        There isn't any tax on it,
        So just relax on it—
If you want trouble double-crossed.
        Don't give in to a frown;
        Turn that frown upside-down,
And get yourself that long face lost!

# ONE LIFE TO LIVE

LADY IN THE DARK (1941). Music, Kurt Weill. *"Allegretto commodo."* In the Glamour Dream, while en route to the Seventh Heaven Night Club, Gertrude Lawrence as Liza Elliott orders Danny Kaye as Beekman, her chauffeur, to stop at Columbus Circle. Leaving the Blue Dusenberg and the Blue Picasso, she asks for her Blue Soapbox. She has decided to make a speech. And sings:

There are many minds in circulation
Believing in reincarnation.
    In me you see
    One who doesn't agree.
Challenging all possible affronts,
  I believe I'll only live once,
And I want to make the most of it:
If there's a party I want to be the host of it;
If there's a haunted house I want to be the ghost
        of it;
If I'm in town I want to be the toast of it.

*Refrain*

I say to me ev'ry morning:
You've only one life to live,
    So why be done in?
    Let's let the sun in,
And gloom can jump in the riv'.

No use to beat on the doldrums;
Let's be imaginative.
    Each day is numbered—
    No good when slumbered—
With only one life to live.

Why let the goblins upset you?
    One smile and see how they run.
And what does worrying net you?
        Nothing!
        *Tha* thing
Is to have fun.


All this may sound kind of hackneyed,
But it's the best I can give.
    Soon comes December,
    So, please remember
You've only one life to live,
Just—one life to live.


### Second Refrain

#### Beekman

She says to her ev'ry morning:
She's only one life to live;
    No time like Now-time
    For that big Wow-time,
And gloom can jump in the riv'.


#### Liza

What you collect at the grindstone
Becomes a millstone in time.
    This is my thesis:
    Why go to pieces?
Step out while you're in your prime.


They may say I'm an escapist,
    But I would rather, by far,
Be that than be a red tape-ist.
        Lead me,
        Speed me
Straight to the bar!

> Just laugh at Old Man Repression—
> He'll fade out into obliv'—
> And you're the winner!
> > (*Beekman points to his wrist watch*)
> I'm off to dinner!
> I've only one life to live,
> Just—one life to live.

---

*I Am Ungallant.* Kurt's style direction for this song is *"Allegretto commodo."* In Scholes's *Oxford Companion to Music, "Allegretto"* is defined as "Pretty lively," and *"Commodo"* as " 'Convenient,' i.e., without any suspicion of strain." Which gives me a fairly lively and convenient lead to say there was no suspicion of strain in Miss Lawrence's fondness for, and acceptance of, not only the dramatic but also the musical portion of her role. And after we opened, there were no reservations in the tremendous acclaim this gifted actress received from the critics and the public for her performance—whether in any of her dramatic scenes or in any of her numbers. Yet, after a while—although "One Life to Live" got over as well as ever on stage—off stage, Gertie found some suspicion of strain in it, much discussion *allegretto* resulting.

Some four months after the opening, Kurt wrote me, May 28, '41: "Gertie asked me if there is any possibility that we write her a new song instead of 'One life to live.' . . . I dismissed it the first few times she talked about it, but she keeps nagging and I finally told her I would get in touch with you. . . . The funny thing is that she is doing 'One life to live' much better now and that it gets the biggest hand next to 'Jenny' and 'Tschaikowsky.' " Kurt was willing to oblige, but collaboration by mail would have been unsatisfactory; and I didn't fancy going to New York for three weeks or more to work on replacing a number which was doing all right, and which perhaps we couldn't better. There was further correspondence until the show closed for the summer, when Gertie and "One Life to Live" took vacations.

Then, rehearsals again, and *Lady* reopened. Kurt, Sept. 9:

"She keeps on kicking about 'One life to live' (which, by the way, gets a very good hand every night). She says it is just an ice-breaker [indeed!] and she has to work hard to get anything out of it, and what she needs at this moment is a funny song . . . because that would make the whole first act easier for her. . . . I thought she had forgotten it, but she started again and in one rehearsal she got a fit and said, any other actress in her place would just demand a new song and it is not her fault that I cannot get together with the lyric writer etc. etc. Last week she said she would be perfectly happy if you could write a new lyric to the tune of 'Bats about you' [a discarded number]. . . . She suggested to keep the same verse we have now for 'One life to live' and then go into the new song. Well, Moss and I promised her to get in touch with you. . . ."

From me to Kurt, Sept. 29: "I figured the longer I took answering you—or rather, not answering you—the more louse I would be and the more you could blame me. . . . Of all the thankless jobs in show business—to be asked to write a new song for a hit which is in its second season. . . . If, as you say, the show makes too many demands on her physically mightn't it be a good idea to lighten her burden somewhat and cut the number down or even cut the whole number out. . . . [Then, a switch:] If she is still adamant and kicking, I suppose something will have to be done. Next week I'll start thinking about her problem [mine, mostly]. I'm hoping, though, you write me that she has entirely forgotten the issue." And apparently she had, because on Oct. 22 I was able to write: "The news is good especially about Gertie seemingly having forgotten that she wanted a song to replace 'One Life to Live.' "

Two years later, in the fall of '43, when *Lady* played Los Angeles (with Gertie as enchanting as ever and "One Life to Live" still getting a good hand), I went backstage to say hello. Since the days of *Oh, Kay!* Gertie had always been pleasantly cordial to me and was being so to a dozen visitors when I entered her dressing room. But my hello received so reluctant and lukewarm a response that about a minute and a half later I found myself taxiing back to Beverly Hills and wondering if Kurt and I were right about her "seemingly having forgotten."

# SLAP THAT BASS

SHALL WE DANCE (1937). Music, George Gershwin. "Rhyth-mically." Fred Astaire, against the background of a transatlantic-liner engine room, and to the cadence of its pulsating machinery.

Zoom—zoom, zoom—zoom,
The world is in a mess.
 With politics and taxes
 And people grinding axes,
There's no happiness.

Zoom—zoom, zoom—zoom,
Rhythm, lead your ace!
 The future doesn't fret me
 If I can only get me
Someone to slap that bass.

Happiness is not a riddle
When I'm list'ning to that big bass fiddle.

*Refrain*

Slap that bass—
Slap it till it's dizzy.
Slap that bass—
Keep the rhythm busy.
 Zoom, zoom, zoom—
Misery—you got to go.

Slap that bass—
Use it like a tonic.
Slap that bass—
Keep your Philharmonic.
 Zoom, zoom, zoom—
And the milk and honey'll flow!

Dictators would be better off
If they zoom-zoomed now and then;
Today you can see that the happiest men
    All got rhythm.

In which case,
If you want to bubble—
    Slap that bass;
Slap away your trouble.
Learn to zoom, zoom, zoom—
    Slap that bass!

---

*Embarrassing Moment.* Sunday nights at the old Trocadero Club in Hollywood were a sort of showcase for new and generally unknown talent the various studios had just signed. I was there the night a little thirteen-year-old-girl singer from MGM, accompanied at the piano by her bespectacled mother, was cheered by the professional audience after each of three songs. Then came the announcement that Miss Judy Garland's next number would be "Slap That Bass." Startled, I turned to producer Pandro Berman with a look that could mean only: "What's *this?* Where'd she get *that?*" (All the work on the film *Shall We Dance* hadn't as yet been completed; "Slap That Bass" was in, but, other than those at our table, who knew it?)

Judy hadn't sung eight bars before we again gave one another looks of "What's *this?*" It wasn't our number at all. Soon one table companion grinned at me; another winked—intimating wasn't I the sly one trying to put over someone else's title. I was not only embarrassed but concerned; perhaps a new effort was in order, so I paid little attention to the rest of the program. By the time we left, however, reason had overcome fluster. You can't copyright titles, and other than the title the two songs had nothing whatever in common. So our "Slap That Bass" stayed put.

✳     ✳     ✳

Over the years several million songs have been published; and since titles as such aren't copyrightable, identicals among them are bound to occur. Now and then there is a plagiarism suit, but these are usually based on the melodic line—scarcely ever on lyric line or title. (See note to "Shall We Dance.") But if damage or possible harm—not merely vanity or irritation—is at stake (e.g., if someone had the temerity to publish a new song called "Old Man River") it's more than likely the courts could estop the Johnny-come-lately.

# STRIKE UP THE BAND

STRIKE UP THE BAND (1927). Music, George Gershwin. "In slow March time." Sung by Jim Townsend, Jerry Goff, with parenthetical sounds by the Ensemble.

> Let the drums roll out!
>  (Boom boom boom!)
> Let the trumpet call!
>  (Ta-ta-ra-ta-ta-ta-ta!)
> While the people shout
>  (Hooray!)
> Strike up the band!
>
> Hear the cymbals ring!
>  (Tszing-tszing-tszing!)
> Calling one and all
>  (Ta-ta-ra-ta-ta-ta-ta!)
> To the martial swing,
>  (Left, right!)
> Strike up the band!
>
> There is work to be done, to be done—
> There's a war to be won, to be won—
> Come you son of a son of a gun—
>  Take your stand!
>
> Fall in line, yea bo—
> Come along, let's go!
> Hey, leader, STRIKE UP THE BAND!

---

*The Fifth Try.* Late one weekend night in the spring of 1927, I got to my hotel room with the Sunday papers. I looked for a slit of light under the door of the adjoining room—but no light, so I figured my brother was asleep. (We were in Atlantic City for *Strike Up the Band* discussions with producer Edgar Selwyn.) I hadn't finished the paper's first section when the lights went up in the next room; its door opened and my pajamaed brother appeared. "I thought you were asleep," I said. "No, I've been lying in bed thinking, and I think I've got it." "Got what?" I asked. "Why, the march, of course. I think I've finally got it. Come on in." It was off-season and, with no guests to disturb within ten rooms of us, the hotel had sent up a piano. I sat down near the upright and said: "I hope you've *really* finally made up your mind." He played the refrain of the march practically as it is known today. Did I like it? Certainly I liked it, but— "But what?" "Are you sure you won't change your mind again?" "Yes, I'm pretty sure this time." "That's good. Don't forget it." By this last remark I meant not only the new tune but also an implied guarantee that he wouldn't try for another.

The reason I wanted assurance was that over the weeks he had written four different marches and on each occasion I had responded with "That's fine. Just right. O.K., I'll write it up." And each time I had received the same answer: "Not bad, but not yet. Don't worry. I'll remember it; but it's for an important spot, and maybe I'll get something better."

This fifth try turned out to be it. Interestingly enough, the earlier four had been written at the piano; the fifth and final came to him while lying in bed.

$$* \quad * \quad *$$

*The Four Verses.* There are four published versions of this song. The music remains the same in all of them, but the words of the verse have been revised several times. The first published version (1927) was the one sung in the show:

> We fought in nineteen-seventeen,
> > Rum-ta-ta tum-tum-tum!
> And drove the tyrant from the scene,
> > Rum-ta-ta tum-tum-tum!

We're in a bigger, better war
    For your patriotic pastime.
We don't know what we're fighting for—
    But we didn't know the last time!

So, load the cannon! Draw the blade!
    Rum-ta-ta tum-tum-tum!
Come on, and join the Big Parade!
Rum-ta-ta tum-tum, Rum-ta-ta tum-tum,
    Rum-ta-ta tum-tum-tum!

That was written in a comparatively peaceful period when there was much talk and some action among nations about disarmament.

Thirteen years later (1940), with another World War in the offing, it would have been unpatriotic not to have changed the sentiment of the "pastime—last time" quatrain; so an edition was published with these lines.

We hope there'll be no other war,
    But if we are forced into one—
The flag that we'll be fighting for
    Is the Red and White and Blue one!

(The standard version today.)

Two years later (1942), after we had been forced into World War II, this became:

Again the Hun is at the gate
    For his customary pastime;
Again he sings his Hymn of Hate—
    But we'll make this time the last time!

(This version is out of print now—I hope.)

Another version was published between the 1927 and 1940 ones—this, with a completely rewritten lyric called "Strike Up the Band for U.C.L.A." In 1936 I was asked to adapt "Strike Up" so that it could be included among the college songs of the University of California at Los Angeles, to be used particularly at football games. And for over twenty years I have been the recipient annually of a rather unusual song royalty or dividend: two season passes to the home football games.

# Ladies in Lament

*"Boy! What Love Has Done to Me!"*

*"But Not for Me"*

*"In the Mandarin's Orchid Garden"*

*"Jilted, Jilted!"*

*"The Man That Got Away"*

*"Words without Music"*

# BOY! WHAT LOVE HAS DONE TO ME!

GIRL CRAZY (1930). Music, George Gershwin. "Rather slow, sorrowfully." Ethel Merman as Kate Fothergill, wife of a petty gambler, tells what it's like.

1

I fetch his slippers,
Fill up the pipe he smokes,
Join up with gyppers,
Laugh at his oldest jokes;
Yet here I anchor—
I might have had a banker—
Boy! What love has done to me!

His nature's funny—
Quarrelsome half the time;
And as for money,
He hasn't got a dime.
And here's the joker:
I might have had a broker.
Boy! What love has done to me!

When a guy looks my way,
Does he get emphatic?
Say, he gets dramatic!
I just want to fly 'way—
But if I left him I'd be all at sea.

I'm just his slavey;
Life is a funny thing.
He gets the gravy,
I got a wedding ring.
And still I love him,
There's nobody above him—
Boy! What love has done to me!

2

His brains are minus,
Never a thought in sight—
And yet his highness
Lectures me day and night;
Oh, where was my sense
To sign that wedding license?
Boy! What love has done to me!

My life he's wrecking;
Bet you could find him now
Out somewhere necking
Somebody else's frau.
You get to know life
When married to a low-life—
Boy! What love has done to me!

I can't hold my head up:
The butcher, the baker,
All know he's a faker;
Brother, I am fed up—
But if I left him he'd be up a tree.

Where will I wind up?
I don't know where I'm at.
I make my mind up
I ought to leave him flat.
But I have grown so
I love the dirty so'n'so!
Boy! What love has done to me!

## Ladies in Lament

This was one of three *Girl Crazy* songs—the other two: "I Got Rhythm," "Sam and Delilah"—written for Frisco Kate, a role played by the dynamic Ethel Merman. Although this young woman was appearing for the first time on any stage, her assurance, timing, and delivery, both as comedienne and singer—with a no-nonsense voice that could reach not only standees but ticket-takers in the lobby—convinced the opening-night audience that it was witnessing the discovery of a new star.

*Girl Crazy* was a lively show. Willie Howard was at his funniest as a New York taxi-driver become sheriff in a Western town; the dancing was novel; the score featured, in addition to the Merman songs, "Embraceable You," "Bidin' My Time," and "But Not for Me"; and I am told the hep pit orchestra, conducted by Red Nichols, included many instrumentalists who later became famous in the jazz world. All in all, this musical, which ran thirty-four weeks, was considered a hit. Thirty-four weeks, these days, wouldn't be considered much of a run; but for those depression days when the national income was about one tenth of what it is now, one couldn't complain.

*   *   *

*Additional Note Written about a Year Later.* As lyricist I had nothing to do with the pit orchestra except to listen and take for granted their excellence—concerned only that the playing wouldn't be too loud. (From an unfinished lyric: "When the orchestra drowns the singers / And the singers drown the words . . .") The musicians were usually selected—still are, I imagine—after discussions among composer, conductor, producer, and the union contractor. Recently I have been able to obtain the names of some of the *Girl Crazy* pitmen from film producer Roger Edens, who was on-stage pianist for Miss Merman in the Western bar scene. Among them: Benny Goodman, Gene Krupa, Glenn Miller, Jack Teagarden, Jimmy Dorsey.

233

# BUT NOT FOR ME

CRAZY GIRL (1930). Music, George Gershwin. "Pessimistically and rather slowly." Sung by postmistress Molly Gray (Ginger Rogers) after the customary lovers' quarrel in Act II.

> Old Man Sunshine—listen, you!
> Never tell me Dreams Come True!
>     Just try it—
>     And I'll start a riot.
> Beatrice Fairfax—don't you dare
> Ever tell me he will care;
>     I'm certain
>     It's the Final Curtain.
> I never want to hear
> From any cheer-
>     Ful Pollyannas,
> Who tell you Fate
> Supplies a Mate—
>     It's all bananas!

> *Refrain*
>
> They're writing songs of love,
>     But not for me;
> A lucky star's above,
>     But not for me.
>
> With Love to Lead the Way,
> I've found more Clouds of Gray
> Than any Russian play
>     Could guarantee.
>
> I was a fool to fall
>     And Get That Way;
> Heigh ho! Alas! and al-
>     So, Lackaday!

## Ladies in Lament

Although I can't dismiss
The mem'ry of his kiss—
    I guess he's not for me.

### Second Refrain

He's knocking on a door,
    But not for me;
He'll plan a two by four,
    But not for me.

I know that Love's a Game;
I'm puzzled, just the same—
Was I the Moth or Flame . . . ?
    I'm all at sea.

It all began so well,
    But what an end!
This is the time a Fell-
    Er Needs a Friend:

When ev'ry happy plot
Ends with the marriage knot—
    And there's no knot for me.

---

*Notes for Teenagers.* Beatrice Fairfax was one of the earliest Advice-to-the-Lovelorn columnists. . . . Using "a feller needs a friend" was a tangential tribute to the hundreds of nostalgic cartoons of boyhood by Clare Briggs (1875–1930), headed "When a Feller Needs a Friend." . . . The title of Eleanor H. Porter's 1913 novel, *Pollyanna,* is still with us as a term of excessive optimism. . . . "Bananas" as a pejorative term implying disbelief was one of many slang terms started by sports-writer and cartoonist Thomas Aloysius Dorgan (1877–1929), "Tad." . . . The "two by four" wasn't the hyphenated two-by-four piece of lumber. Rather, as sung here and elsewhere, it meant a dream house for two ("and baby makes three").

\*     \*     \*

*A Brief Concordance.* I see that in this category "But Not for Me" is one of two lyrics whose titles contain the pronoun *me*. Excluding two-letter prepositions and "an," I imagine *me* is the most used two-letter word in Songdom. "I" (leaving out indefinite article "a") is doubtless the most used one-letter word (and everywhere else, for that matter). "You" (if definite article "the" bows out) is the most frequent three-letter word. "Love" probably gets the four-letter nod (referring strictly to songs that can be heard in the home). In the five-letter stakes I would wager that "heart" and "dream" photo-finish in a dead heat. As for words of more than five letters, you're on your own.

# IN THE MANDARIN'S ORCHID
# GARDEN

Written in 1929 for *East Is West*. Music, George Gershwin. *"Allegro moderato."* For a Sing-Song Girl.

>Somehow by fate misguided,
>A buttercup resided
>In The Mandarin's Orchid Garden—
>A buttercup that did not grace
>The loveliness of such a place.
>And so it simply shriveled up
>And begged each orchid's pardon.
>Poor little buttercup in The Orchid Garden. . . .
>
>I, too, have been misguided.
>Too long have I resided
>In The Mandarin's Orchid Garden.
>And though for friendliness I yearn,
>I do not know which way to turn.
>How long must I keep shriv'ling up
>And beg each lady's pardon?
>A lonely buttercup in The Orchid Garden.

---

*Recitation.* "Orchid Garden" was to be sung by a Sing-Song Girl at one side of the stage—as a vocal accompaniment to a Chinese ballet on full stage. When *East Is West* had to be abandoned by Ziegfeld, our music-publisher salvaged this unsung Sing-Song Girl lament and published it, feeling that some concert artists would take to it. But, so far as I know, only one used it—Eleanor Marum, in four or five recitals. A couple of years later, though, I found that it had an existence, however fleeting, in another form.

One night on our first trip to Hollywood we were dinner guests at the Bel-Air home of one of the studio's executives. After I was introduced to the gracious hostess, his wife, she took me aside and recited a few lines, starting with "Somehow by fate misguided, / A buttercup resided . . ." Vastly surprised, since the song had sold only a few copies, and wondering how it had traveled twenty-six hundred miles to Bel-Air, I said: "I didn't know anyone knew that song. How did you happen to learn it?" "Oh," she replied, "I can't play it—only recite it. You see, I take elocution lessons and my teacher gave me the words to learn."

Just then dinner was announced, and I never did find out who the elocution teacher was—nor why he, or she, had got hold of a copy to put it to this rather unlikely use.

# JILTED, JILTED!

OF THEE I SING (1931). Music, George Gershwin. *"Allegro."* Act II, scene iii. The Senate. Impeachment Trial of President Wintergreen. He has married his secretary instead of Diana Devereaux, the beauty-contest winner chosen to be his bride. Since Diana is of French descent, she is accompanied by the French Ambassador. Sung by Grace Brinkley, Florenz Ames, and Senators.

*French Ambassador (recitativo)*
Tell your story, little one. *Commencez, s'il vous plait.*

*Diana*

    Jilted, jilted,
I'm a flow'r that's wilted;
    Blighted, blighted,
Till the wrong is righted;

    Broken, broken,
By a man soft-spoken;
    Faded, faded—
Heaven knows why!

When men are deceivers, I'm afraid
'Tis sad to be a trusting maid.

    Jilted, jilted, jilted am I . . .
Oh, what is there left but to die.
    *Senate (visibly affected)*
Jilted, jilted, jilted is she . . .
Oh, what is there left but—to dee!

*All*
Boo-hoo! Boo-hoo! Boo-hoo!

The Senate was not only visibly affected by this touching waltz, but suddenly became Scotsmen for no reason except rhyme.

\*       \*       \*

Later in the scene the French Ambassador, denouncing Wintergreen, sang:

> You've dealt a lovely maid
> A blow that is injurious;
> A very dirty trick was played—
> And France is simply furious!

And, in a reprise of "The Illegitimate Daughter," won absolute sympathy for Diana with:

> She's contemplating suicide
> Because that man he threw aside
> A lady with the blue blood of Napoleon. . . .

But all in vain. The Senate was within a few votes of convicting the President when Mrs. Wintergreen rushed on and announced (in ¾ time and high soprano) her husband's delicate condition, explaining:

> I'm about to be a mother,
> He's about to be a father;
> We're about to have a baby. . . .

Which completely changed the picture. The Senate instanter dropped the impeachment proceedings and, as a man, rushed to congratulate the expectant father, leaving poor Diana again in the lurch.

# THE MAN THAT GOT AWAY

A STAR IS BORN (1954). Music, Harold Arlen. "Slowly, with a steady insistence." Judy Garland as Esther Blodgett, girl singer with a band, in a Sunset Strip musicians' hangout, after hours.

> The night is bitter,
> The stars have lost their glitter;
> The winds grow colder
> And suddenly you're older—
> And all because of the man that got away.

> No more his eager call,
> The writing's on the wall;
> The dreams you've dreamed have all
> Gone astray.

> The man that won you
> Has run off and undone you.
> That great beginning
> Has seen the final inning.
> Don't know what happened. It's all a crazy game.

> No more that all-time thrill,
> For you've been through the mill—
> And never a new love will
> Be the same.

> Good riddance, good bye!
> Ev'ry trick of his you're on to.
> But, fools will be fools—
> And where's he gone to?

> The road gets rougher,
> It's lonelier and tougher.
> With hope you burn up—
> Tomorrow he may turn up.
> There's just no let-up the live-long night and day.

Ever since this world began
There is nothing sadder than
A one man woman looking for
The man that got away . . .
The man that got away.

---

Some movie-reviewers, in noticing this number, called it "The Man Who Got Away"—a whodunit title I wouldn't have considered a lyric possibility. The change, whether deliberate or unwitting, was made by those who obviously prefer "who" to "that" when the relative pronoun refers to Homo sapiens, or any reasonable facsimile thereof. Generally, of course, my syntactical course would follow theirs. But this had to be "The Man *That* Got Away" because, actually, the title hit me as a paraphrase of the angler's "You should have seen the one that got away."

\*      \*      \*

The word "man" in a title ("My Man," "A Good Man Is Hard to Find"—hundreds of others) usually limits the rendition of a song to female vocalists. There would be much contracting-of-brow and looking-askance if a male singer attempted: "Some day he'll come along / The man I love. . . ." And if he tried mere gender-changing, some undesirable attributes could emerge—Amazonian here, for instance:

Some day she'll come along,
The girl I love;
And she'll be big and strong. . . .

Opposite-sex versions of such lyrics being rare, it was consequently a surprise when Frank Sinatra telephoned me he wanted to do a recording called "The *Gal* That Got Away." He pointed out that, outside of the concluding lines, the lyric required only a change of pronoun: "No more his eager call" to "her eager call," &c. That sounding likely, I improvised this ending:

## Ladies in Lament

Ever since this world began
There is nothing sadder than
A lost, lost loser looking for
The gal that got away.

Which alliterative line he liked and wrote down. His excellent recording resulted, and "The Gal That Got Away" got away with it.
But, again: a sex transilience of this sort is unusual.

$$* \qquad * \qquad *$$

When the composer of this song visited me a year ago and found
I'd actually started working on this book, he insisted on having
something of his included among the notes. I said: "O.K., Harold.
What'll you write about?" He said: "I'll think of something."

Recently he sent me a piece, dictated by him in New York. I
find it charming. The characters, in the order of their appearance,
are:

Ira—lyricist of the film *A Star Is Born.*
Moss—Moss Hart, screenwriter of ditto.
Judy—Judy Garland, star of ditto.
Sid—Sid Luft, Judy's husband and producer of the film.
Kitty—Kitty Carlisle, Mrs. Hart.

Somehow my contributor overlooked dictating a title. I'll call it:

### My Broken Promise
*by Harold Arlen*

WE had been working about two weeks on *A Star Is Born* and
—luckily—somehow or other we'd got the first two songs
done. (That was "Gotta Have Me Go with You" and "The
Man That Got Away.") We were at it every afternoon, and I
wanted to go away for the weekend. "Ira, I want to go to Palm
Springs." "Don't." "Why not?" "Well, Moss is there, and Judy
is there, and you'll be playing the songs for them and it's

much too early." And he was as vehement as Ira can get. He said: "You'll spoil things." I said: "Ira, I promise you. I'm not going there to see Moss and Judy; I just want a break."

I went up to that golf course where Ben Hogan was the pro —the Tamarisk—and I went out that Saturday morning. Because I wasn't feeling too well, I wasn't supposed to play. But I saw Judy and Sid, large as life, just teeing off. I said: "I'll walk around with you." Nobody said anything about the picture. Then about the middle of the round (I'd be trailing them, and then be ahead of them, and they'd catch up, and then I'd trail them again) I started to whistle, very softly. I don't know what tempted me. She was about twenty yards away—it was a kind of a tease and I couldn't stand it. I love Ira and I love Judy, and, well, I just whistled the main phrase of "The Man That Got Away." Suddenly, third or fourth whistle, Judy turned around. "Harold, what are you whistling?" "Nothing. I don't know." This continued. "Harold, what *are* you whistling? Don't tell me it's something from the picture." I said no. "Harold, I've got an idea it *must* be from the picture—don't hold out on me." Finally, on the eighteenth hole, Sid hit the ball 320 yards into the sand trap, and while he dug it out, Judy insisted: "Harold, there's a piano in the clubhouse, and you've *got* to play it." I kept playing it down: "It's just something we've been working on. I don't know how well you'll like it." So I played both songs, and— well—they were the first songs, the script wasn't finished, it was their first picture—and they went wild with joy. "Ira, Smira, he'll be happy about it," I thought. So I went to see Moss and Kitty. Same thing. They wanted to call Ira. I said: "Oh, don't! I've promised him not to play them." But they insisted and phoned Ira and said how wonderful it was, and he was delighted. And when I came back he was beaming and never said a word about my broken promise.

# WORDS WITHOUT MUSIC

ZIEGFELD FOLLIES OF 1936. Music, Vernon Duke. Verse: *"Tranquillo";* refrain: *"Molto espressivo."* Sung by Gertrude Niesen. A Surrealist Ballet, Harriet Hoctor and Corps de Ballet; setting by Vincente Minnelli, choreography by George Balanchine.

It's an old, old, old variation
On the very oldest of themes:
It's the one that starts as flirtation
And that ends in broken dreams;
It's the feeling when he enfolds you
He'll forget you soon as he's gone—
But, what can you do?
You're in love and you
Hold on.

### Refrain

Words without music,
Smoke without flame—
Charming phrases
That sing your praises
And call your name.

Nights without magic,
Days without end—
Same old story,
The empty glory
Of Let's Pretend.

Had I had an inkling
That he could not be true,
These blues of mine could never start;
But, stars above were twinkling,
And then before I knew—
He was locked up in my heart.

245

I'll hear words without music
All my life long—
Hoping, praying
That what he's saying
Will turn to song.

---

You can count on the fingers of one hand, and perhaps the thumb and index finger of the other, the number of our theater composers whose melodic line and harmonies are highly individual. There is no question but that Vernon Duke must be considered one of these. Although "Words without Music" is scarcely known— and therefore not in the class of "April in Paris," "Autumn in New York," "I Can't Get Started," "What Is There to Say?" and many others—it is an excellent example of Duke's distinctive style.

\*     \*     \*

*Excerpts from a Diary.* When Vernon Duke was working on his autobiography, *Passport to Paris,* he asked me whether my brother and/or I had saved any of his letters. I was able to find about a dozen letters and postcards which I believe helped him to some extent with places, dates, and events. Then I remembered a European diary I had kept in 1928 and that one day in Paris Vernon had dropped in on us at the Hotel Majestic. I found the diary, located the page on which he was mentioned, read it, and told him he could have it for his book, on condition that he include not only the first paragraph but also the second of that day's report. Vernon agreed that he would put both in, but when the book was published I found he had used only the first paragraph. This:

Paris, April 6th Friday (Weather—sunshine at last). Letter from Selwyn to George saying "Strike Up the Band" would be done next season. All of us happy about it. Dukelsky came in for an hour or so. Argued with George about parts of "American in Paris" saying that George was 1928 in his musi-

cal comedies and in most of his concert music but that in
"A.I.P." he allowed himself to become saccharine in
spots. When he left, Walton, an English composer friend of
George's and Dukelsky's in London came in. Played us a
parody waltz, a tune and part of his symphony which had
been done recently by Koussevitzky. All pretty bad. Walton
told George to disregard Dukelsky's advice as Duke was influenced by Prokofiev and thought anyone who wrote in another style old-fashioned; also, that nothing of Duke's had become popular, &c., &c. Most interesting what they all think of
one another.

The second paragraph was a report of a conversation about a
party given for us the night before by Polish-French composer
Alexandre Tansman. Since Vernon promised to, but didn't, in-
corporate it in his book, I feel free now to offer the world this
hitherto undisclosed critical disclosure:

G. had told Duke about the party at Tansman's. Duke:
"Tansman? A second rater who will never amount to anything. Who was there?" George: "Rieti, the Italian." Duke:
"Very good." G.: "E. Robert Schmitz." Duke: "Very good."
G.: "Ibert." Duke sniffed, "Second rate." George: "Petit, the
critic." Duke: "Not important—third rate." George went
through some more names, Duke sniffing all the while. Then
he said, "You shouldn't have gone to that party. It will hurt
you, people like that. A dozen people there, but only two,
really, Rieti and Schmitz."

✳   ✳   ✳

*Apology to Sir William.* George found Walton's music that day
more interesting than I did. I realize my snap judgment was
based not so much on what was being played as on its performance.
I was so accustomed to George's brilliant pianism and rich harmonies that Walton's rather delicate playing and offerings suffered
by comparison.

Similarly, as a matter of truth—after collaborating with Vernon on the *Follies* most of 1935 and listening to *his* rich playing and lush harmonies, I wondered what had happened to my brother (or to me) when I began working with George again. The first song we were trying to lick was the eether-eyether notion ("Let's Call the Whole Thing Off"), and I nodded approval at the tune and rhythm he favored. Inwardly, though, I was bothered. The tune seemed thin and unimportant, and for a day or two I felt I was being fed a sparser musical diet than with Duke. Then, gradually, notes began to fill out and rhythms sparkle.

# Sound Effects

*" 'S Wonderful"*

*"Applause, Applause!"*

*"They All Laughed"*

*"Do, Do, Do"*

*"Let's Call the Whole Thing Off"*

# 'S WONDERFUL

FUNNY FACE (1927). Music, George Gershwin. "Liltingly."
Adele Astaire was Frankie, Allen Kearns was Peter.

*Peter*

Life has just begun:
Jack has found his Jill.
Don't know what you've done,
But I'm all a-thrill.
How can words express
Your divine appeal?
You could never guess
All the love I feel.
From now on, lady, I insist,
For me no other girls exist.

*Refrain*

'S wonderful! 'S marvelous—
    You should care for me!
'S awful nice! 'S Paradise—
    'S what I love to see!
You've made my life so glamorous,
You can't blame me for feeling amorous.
    Oh, 's wonderful! 'S marvelous—
    That you should care for me!

### Frankie

Don't mind telling you,
In my humble fash,
That you thrill me through
With a tender pash.
When you said you care,
'Magine my emosh;
I swore, then and there,
Permanent devosh.
You made all other boys seem blah;
Just you alone filled me with AAH!

### Refrain

'S wonderful! 'S marvelous—
    You should care for me!
'S awful nice! 'S Paradise—
    'S what I love to see!
My dear, it's four leaf clover time;
From now on my heart's working overtime.
    Oh, 's wonderful! 'S marvelous—
    That you should care for me!

---

The principal reason for writing this lyric was to feature the sibilant sound effect by deleting the "it" of "it's" and slurring the leftover "s" with the first syllable of the following word. So I'm frequently baffled by what some singers have in mind and throat when they formalize the phrases to *"It's* wonderful," *"It's* marvelous," *"It's* Paradise," &c.

Re "fash," "pash," "emosh," and "devosh" in the second verse: I had heard comedian Walter Catlett in *Lady, Be Good!* clipping syllables from some favored words, so thought it would be novel to adopt this device in a song. I used it first in "Sunny Disposish," written with composer Phil Charig for *Americana.* (A few years later I came across some light verse by England's Captain

Harry Graham to discover that he had specialized in this lopping-off device long before me.)

*The Proper Twenties.* In Philadelphia, where *Funny Face* opened, one of the town's top-critics saw me one afternoon in the lobby of the Shubert Theatre (a rehearsal was going on inside) and stopped to ask how the changes in the show were coming along. He then wondered if I had done anything about " 'S Wonderful," which, it developed, he thought contained an obscene phrase. I don't know what he would think about it these Freedom-of-Four-Letter-Speech days, but at that time he felt that "feeling amorous" was something better scrawled in chalk than sung from a stage.

# APPLAUSE, APPLAUSE! *

GIVE A GIRL A BREAK (1953). Music, Burton Lane. Finale of the revue within the film. Sung by Gower Champion and Debbie Reynolds.

When the voodoo drum is drumming
Or the humming bird is humming,
Does it thrill you? Does it fill you with delight?
To continue with our jingle:
Are you one of those who tingle
To your shoes-ies at the blues-ies in the night?
Oh, the sounds of bugles calling
Or Niag'ra Falls a-falling
May enchant you—we will grant you that they might;
But for us on the stage, oh brother!
There's just one sound and no other:

*Refrain*

Applause, applause!
We like applause because
It means when it is striking us
The audience is liking us.

Our work demands
You don't sit on your hands—
And if the hand's tremendous,
You send us!

We live, we thrive,
You keep us all alive
With "Bravo!" and "Bravissimo!"
We're dead if it's *pianissimo*.

## Sound Effects

Our quirk is work,
Is work we never shirk
In a happyland of tinsel and gauze,
Because—we like applause!

### Patter Verse

Whether you're a Swiss bell ringer
Or a crooner or a singer
Or monologist, ventriloquist or what—
Or a dog act or magician
Or a musical saw musician
Or an ingenue or pianist who is hot—
Whether you play Punchinello,
Little Eva or Othello—
Having heard the call, you've given all you've got.
And what better reward for a trouper
Than the sound we consider super?

### Second Refrain

Applause, applause!
Vociferous applause
From orchestra to gallery
Could mean a raise in salary.

Give out, give in!—
Be noisy, make a din!
(The manager, he audits
Our plaudits.)

We won renown
When opening out of town;
(In Boston and in Rockaway
They heard applause a block away)—

If we've come through,
Give credit where it's due,
And obey the theater's unwritten laws,
Because—we like applause!

255

*Constructive Criticism.* Although this lyric makes a plea for hand-made appreciation from an audience, it evoked little, if any. Unhappily, the backstage film musical *Give a Girl a Break* got few breaks from the press. True, the picture was nowhere near Academy Award nomination, but it wasn't this bad: On leaving the studio projection room after seeing a rough cut of the film, my wife asked me if I owned any stock in the film company. I told her I had bought several hundred shares the previous year. "Sell it," she said. Being a dutiful husband and California a community-property state, I called my broker next morning and sold. (I lost five hundred dollars by this acquiescence—a month later there could have been a profit—but my action demonstrates (A) that I am a dutiful husband; (B) that something more effective than verbal criticism can be accomplished through the facilities of the New York Stock Exchange.)

\*      \*      \*

*Giving Girls (and Other Females) Titular Breaks.* One of the first shows to be labeled "musical comedy" (a term which emerged in London in the 1890's) was the successful *A Gaiety Girl.* Should anyone interest himself in a study of musical-comedy titles from that time on (why anyone would is beyond me), I'm sure he could prove that the uses of Girl, Lady, Miss, and other female classifications (plus given names like Sally; Irene, Nanette, &c.) vastly outnumber the male variations and prenames. Obviously the entitled female is not Kipling's "a rag and a bone and a hank of hair," but an attractive and potential box-office come-on. No world-shaking thesis this; it's just a sudden awareness of the major number of such uses even in the entertainments I've contributed to: *Two Little Girls in Blue, A Dangerous Maid, The Shocking Miss Pilgrim, Oh, Kay!, Rosalie, Damsel in Distress, Treasure Girl, Cover Girl, Country Girl, Show Girl, That's a Good Girl, Girl Crazy, Lady, Be Good!, Lady in the Dark, My Fair Lady* (this last, of course, not the enormously successful Lerner-Loewe *My Fair Lady,* but the original title on the road and on sheet music of a 1925 musical which for Broadway we renamed *Tell Me More*). The lone marqueed male I've worked for is Porgy and he had to share billing fifty-fifty with Bess.

# THEY ALL LAUGHED

SHALL WE DANCE (1937). Music, George Gershwin. "Gracefully and happily." Sung by Fred Astaire and Ginger Rogers.

The odds were a hundred to one against me,
The world thought the heights were too high to climb.
But people from Missouri never incensed me:
    Oh, I wasn't a bit concerned,
    For from hist'ry I had learned
    How many, many times the worm had turned.

*Refrain*

They all laughed at Christopher Columbus
When he said the world was round;
They all laughed when Edison recorded sound.

They all laughed at Wilbur and his brother
    When they said that man could fly;
       They told Marconi
       Wireless was a phony—
    It's the same old cry!

They laughed at me wanting you,
    Said I was reaching for the moon;
But oh, you came through—
    Now they'll have to change their tune.

They all said we never could be happy,
    They laughed at us—and how!
       But ho, ho, ho—
    Who's got the last laugh now?

*Second Refrain*

They all laughed at Rockefeller Center—
Now they're fighting to get in;
They all laughed at Whitney and his cotton gin.

They all laughed at Fulton and his steamboat,
   Hershey and his choc'late bar.
      Ford and his Lizzie
      Kept the laughers busy—
   That's how people are!

They laughed at me wanting you—
   Said it would be Hello! Good-bye!
But oh, you came through—
   Now they're eating humble pie.

They all said we'd never get together—
   Darling, let's take a bow,
      For ho, ho, ho—
   Who's got the last laugh—
      He, he, he—
   Let's at the past laugh—
      Ha, ha, ha—
   Who's got the last laugh now?

---

In the Twenties not only the stock market but the self-improvement business boomed. One correspondence-school advertisement, for instance, featured "They all laughed when I sat down to play the piano." Along this line, I recall writing a postcard from Paris to Gilbert Gabriel, the drama critic, saying: "They all laughed at the Tour d'Argent last night when I said I would order in French." So the phrase "they all laughed" hibernated and estivated in the back of my mind for a dozen years until the right climate and tune popped it out as a title.

\*　　　\*　　　\*

This lyric is an example of the left-field or circuitous approach to the subject preponderant in Songdom. I believe it was George S.

## Sound Effects

Kaufman (in Hollywood at the time) who, when we played him this one, interrupted us after the lines,

> They told Marconi
> Wireless was a phony—
> It's the same old cry!

and wondered aloud: "Don't tell me this is going to be a love song!" We assured him that that was the intention; and on hearing the catalytic line, "They laughed at me wanting you," he shook his head resignedly and said: "Oh, well."

# DO, DO, DO

OH, KAY! (1926). Music, George Gershwin. "Gracefully." As I recall it, Jimmy (Oscar Shaw), meeting Kay (Gertrude Lawrence) for the first time, kissed her that evening, with no resultant How-dare-you. Here they meet again.

*Jimmy*

I remember the bliss
Of that wonderful kiss.
  I know that a boy
  Could never have more joy
From any little miss.

*Kay*

I remember it quite;
'Twas a wonderful night.

*Jimmy*

Oh, how I'd adore it
If you would encore it. Oh—

*Refrain*

Do, do, do
What you've done, done, done
  Before, Baby.
Do, do, do
What I do, do, do
  Adore, Baby.

Let's try again,
Sigh again,
Fly again to heaven.
  Baby, see
  It's A B C—
I love you and you love me.

## Sound Effects

I know, know, know
What a beau, beau, beau
  Should do, Baby;
So don't, don't, don't
Say it won't, won't, won't
  Come true, Baby.

My heart begins to hum—
Hum de dum de dum-dum-dum,
  So do, do, do
What you've done, done, done
  Before.

---

An hour or so before dinner one evening at our house on 103rd Street I told George that maybe we could do something with the sounds of "do, do" and "done, done." We went up to his studio on the top floor and in half an hour wrote the refrain of the song. (I am certain of the time it took because just as we started to work, my bride-to-be telephoned that she *could* make it for dinner with us; and when she arrived, taxiing in half an hour—less, she says—from Eighth Street, we were able to play her a complete refrain.)

The lyric isn't much to look at, but its sounds of triply repeated syllables were effective over the footlights. The duet was sung with a somewhat faster and steadier beat than would be done today, and came over to the audience with the intended result, a catchy song about a kiss—and nothing else.

I stress this point because the first essay in Sigmund Spaeth's *The Facts of Life in Popular Song* is concerned with suggestive songs, musical-comedy "smart smut," and many songs palpably prurient. In that book musicologist Spaeth turns lyricologist and has made an excellent and frequently amusing study of not only songs of questionable taste, but many other popular-song matters, such as grammar and bad rhymes. Among the suggestive songs he lists "Do, Do, Do," based apparently on this finding: "In the language of Popular Song it is understood that such words as 'hug'

261

and 'kiss' may represent any stage of procreative activity. . . ." If the overtones—and undertones—of a "do, do" and a "done, done" sound-effect effort gave Mr. Spaeth a feeling that some stage of procreative activity was implied, I'm sorry. Whatever may have been hinted at or outspokenly stated in other songs of mine, "Do, Do, Do" was written for its face, not body, value.

(Despite this disclaimer, "Do, Do, Do" can of course be suggestive, if leeringly inflected in husky tones by anyone sexy. But this can be true of anything vocalized in that manner—from the alphabet to the telephone directory to national anthems.)

# LET'S CALL THE WHOLE THING OFF

SHALL WE DANCE (1937). Music, George Gershwin. "Brightly."
Sung and roller-skated by Fred Astaire and Ginger Rogers on the
Mall in Central Park, and why not?

Things have come to a pretty pass—
    Our romance is growing flat,
For you like this and the other,
    While I go for this and that.
Goodness knows what the end will be;
    Oh, I don't know where I'm at. . . .
It looks as if we two will never be one.
Something must be done.

*Refrain*

You say eether and I say eyether,
You say neether and I say nyther;
Eether, eyether, neether, nyther—
    Let's call the whole thing off!

You like potato and I like po-tah-to,
You like tomato and I like to-mah-to;
Potato, po-tah-to, tomato, to-mah-to—
    Let's call the whole thing off!

But oh, if we call the whole thing off, then we must part.
And oh, if we ever part, then that might break my heart.

So, if you like pajamas and I like pa-jah-mas,
I'll wear pajamas and give up pa-jah-mas.
    For we know we
    Need each other, so we
Better call the calling off off.
Let's call the whole thing off!

*Second Refrain*

You say laughter and I say lawfter,
You say after and I say awfter;
Laughter, lawfter, after, awfter—
  Let's call the whole thing off!

You like vanilla and I like vanella,
You, sa's'parilla and I sa's'parella;
Vanilla, vanella, choc'late, strawb'ry—
  Let's call the whole thing off!

But oh, if we call the whole thing off, then we must part.
And oh, if we ever part, then that might break my heart.

  So, if you go for oysters and I go for ersters,
  I'll order oysters and cancel the ersters.
      For we know we
      Need each other, so we
  Better call the calling off off.
  Let's call the whole thing off!

---

Refrain 3 was not in the film, but was given to a young American song-and-dance team to use as an encore in their night-club act—if they had enough breath left:

3

  I say father and you say pater,
  I say mother and you say mater;
  Father, mother, auntie, uncle—
    Let's call the whole thing off!
  I like banana and you like ba-nahn-ah,
  I say Havana and I get Ha-vahn-ah;
  Banana, ba-nahn-ah, Havana, Ha-vahn-ah—
    Never a happy medium!
But oh, &c.
  So, if I go for scallops and you go for lobster,
  No more discussion—we both order lobster.
    For we &c.

\*     \*     \*

## Sound Effects

Many years ago a friend of mine was in London, where, among other activities, he sat in on a couple of chorus-girl calls. At the first audition one of the young ladies gave a copy of this song to the pianist, then sang:

> You say eyether and I say eyether,
> You say nyther and I say nyther;
> Eyether, eyether, nyther, nyther—
> Let's call the whole thing off!

Apparently this sort of thing was quite pronounced that London season. At another audition he listened to a girl doing "Do, Do, Do," but in her pronunciation it became "Doe, Doe, Doe." Evidently she was insistently musical and believed that our repetitive "do" meant the first note of the scale.

\*     \*     \*

Preoccupation with these particular pronunciations must go far back with me, because I still clearly remember the story our 6B teacher in P.S. 20, New York, told the class when she disgressed for a moment in a spelling session. It concerned an American and an Englishman arguing about the correct pronunciation of "neither," with the American insisting on "neether," the Englishman on "nyther." They called on a bystander to settle the dispute: Was it "neether" or "nyther"? "Nayther!" said—who else?—the Irishman.

\*     \*     \*

May I conclude with a note of phonic and marital tolerance on the parts of Mr. and Mrs. Ira Gershwin? We have been married over thirty years, and the pronunciations taught us in our youth still persist: my wife still "eyethers" and "tomahtoes" me, while I "eether" and "tomato" her.

# The Element of Time

*"Bidin' My Time"*

*"Soon"*

*"Long Ago (and Far Away)"*

*"How Long Has This Been Going On?"*

*"For You, For Me, For Evermore"*

*"Love Is Here to Stay"*

# BIDIN' MY TIME

GIRL CRAZY (1930). Music, George Gershwin. "Gracefully."
Sung by The Foursome.

1

Some fellers love to Tip-Toe Through The Tulips;
Some fellers go on Singing In The Rain;
Some fellers keep on Paintin' Skies With Sunshine;
Some fellers keep on Swingin' Down The Lane—
              But—

*Refrain*

I'm Bidin' My Time,
  'Cause that's the kinda guy I'm.
While other folks grow dizzy
I keep busy—
    Bidin' My Time.


Next year, next year,
Somethin's bound to happen;
  This year, this year,
I'll just keep on nappin'—


And—Bidin' My Time,
  'Cause that's the kinda guy I'm.
    There's no regrettin'
    When I'm settin'—
    Bidin' My Time.

269

2

Some fellers love to Tell It To The Daisies;
Some Stroll Beneath The Honeysuckle Vines;
Some fellers when they've Climbed The Highest Mountain
Still keep a-Cryin' For The Carolines—
                    But—

*Refrain*

    I'm Bidin' My Time,
        'Cause that's the kinda guy I'm—
    Beginnin' on a Mond'y
    Right through Sund'y,
        Bidin' My Time.

    Give me, give me
    (A) glass that's full of tinkle;
    Let me, let me
    Dream like Rip Van Winkle.

    He Bided His Time,
    And like that Winkle guy I'm.
        Chasin' 'way flies,
        How the day flies—
        Bidin' My Time!

---

*A Title That Bided Its Time.* At Townsend Harris Hall, the high school then connected with CCNY, I was on the staff of *The Academic Herald* as one of its "Art Editors." As such, I drew some cartoons and department headings; and started a column called "Much Ado." (One semester, I think in 1913, was a prosperous one for the *Herald,* netting an unprecedented profit of almost a hundred dollars. The solution of what to do with this windfall was finally solved by the Editor-in-Chief. He had medals struck off for himself and four or five of the more important editors, and the balance of the money was spent on a spaghetti dinner at Guffanti's for the entire staff of eighteen. We felt rather devilish that night—Chianti was served, even cigars—but most of us were home by ten p.m.)

At City College I collaborated with E. Y. Harburg on a column called "Gargoyle Gargles" for the weekly *Campus;* too, I contributed to the monthly, *Cap and Bells*. Signed "Gersh," the following appeared in the June 1916 issue:

> A desperate deed to do I crave,
>   Beyond all reason and rhyme:
> Some day when I'm feeling especially brave,
>   I'm going to Bide My Time.

Fourteen years after quatrain, with *Girl Crazy* in work, I suggested that "Bidin' My Time" might make a good title for a song in lazy, lethargic mood. (Years earlier I had recollected the phrase and put it down as a possible title. Lyricists usually keep notebooks with titles jotted down from time to time. One day Buddy De Sylva told me that in an hour or two the night before he had put down twenty-two, of which he thought two were probable.) When "Bidin'" was completed, the result was a sixteen-bar verse and thirty-two-bar refrain. Later, in going over the song with my brother, I felt that the refrain was overlong and said: "Let's try cutting out the second eight measures." With the refrain *A A B A* construction becoming *A B A,* this version sounded a bit strange at first; but in a few days the eight-bar scissoring seemed to give the piece a more folksy validity.

"Bidin'" made for a novel quartet in two scenes of the show. Its performance was heightened by the cowboys' (The Foursome) now and then accompanying themselves on the lowly instruments of harmonica, jew's-harp, ocarina, and tin flute.

# SOON

STRIKE UP THE BAND (1930). Music, George Gershwin. "Not fast (with tender expression)." Jim, Jerry Goff, and Joan, Margaret Schilling.

*Jim*

I'm making up for all the years
  That I waited;
  I'm compensated
  At last.
My heart is through with shirking;
Thanks to you it's working
  Fast.
The many lonely nights and days
  When this duffer
  Just had to suffer
  Are past.

*Refrain*

Soon—the lonely nights will be ended;
Soon—two hearts as one will be blended.
I've found the happiness I've waited for:
The only girl that I was fated for.
Oh! Soon—a little cottage will find us
Safe, with all our cares far behind us.
The day you're mine this world will be in tune.
Let's make that day come soon.

*Joan*

Soon—my dear, you'll never be lonely;
Soon—you'll find I live for you only.
When I'm with you who cares what time it is,
Or what the place or what the climate is?
Oh! Soon—our little ship will come sailing
Home, through every storm, never failing.
The day you're mine this world will be in tune.
Let's make that day come soon.

## The Element of Time

In the original version of *Strike Up the Band* there was a longish Act I finale which wound up with the title song, "Strike Up the Band." At one point in this fifteen-minute musical sequence, Jim, our hero, publicly denounced the use of Grade B milk in the manufacture of Fletcher's Chocolate Products. Jim's girl friend, Joan Fletcher, denied the allegation about her father and, to a tune somewhat aria-like, sang:

> Jim—how could you do such a thing?
> Oh, Jim!—Unworthy of you such a thing!

This four-bar bit of melody intrigued some of our friends, who kept insisting this strain could be the basis of a song. We didn't disagree. So, for the new version of the show two and one half years later—"Soon."

# LONG AGO (AND FAR AWAY)

COVER GIRL (1944). Music, Jerome Kern. Verse: *"Con moto —lightly"*; burthen: *"Cantabile."* Sung by Gene Kelly to Rita Hayworth.

> Dreary days are over,
> Life's a four leaf clover.
> Sessions of depressions are through:
> Ev'ry hope I longed for long ago comes true.
>
> *Burthen*
>
> Long ago and far away
> I dreamed a dream one day—
> And now that dream is here beside me.
> Long the skies were overcast,
> But now the clouds have passed:
>     You're here at last!
> Chills run up and down my spine,
> Aladdin's lamp is mine:
> The dream I dreamed was not denied me.
> Just one look and then I knew
> That all I longed for long ago was you.

---

Disregarding the verse (a last-minute rush job), this one took a lot of experimenting. (I have before me a dozen crowded worksheets; there must have been thirty or forty others I tore up at the time.) The smooth, meditative, melodic line brought the problem of where to embed the title. A one-syllable title like "Who?" or "Soon" was possible on the first note of the burthen; one like "Night and Day" or "All Alone" would suit the first three notes; and there were other possibilities—as, observably, the song was finally performed with a five-word seven-syllable title.

In all, I worked on four, maybe five, different lyrics. The second, which used a two-word four-syllable title, wasn't too bad, and Kern liked it a great deal, especially the alliterative last line. It was called "Midnight Music":

> Just a whisper, soft and low,
> And midnight was aglow,
> For oh, your words made midnight music—
> Words that brought me such a thrill
> The echoes haunt me still—
> And always will.
> In that midnight rendezvous
> You said, "There's only you."
> And oh, there never was such music!
> Darkened streets began to shine
> The moment midnight music made you mine.

But no one felt that any of the settings for this tune was a must; nothing was disliked, but no this-is-it enthusiasm was engendered. I seem to remember that the only advice I received at conferences was "Keep it simple, keep it simple."

One day Arthur Schwartz—our composer friend was *Cover Girl*'s producer—telephoned from the studio that this tune had to be recorded in a couple of days. Did I have anything? I mentioned the latest I'd been wrestling with: "Long Ago and Far Away." "Fine. Let's have it." "Now? On the telephone?" "Sure." So I read it to him; he wrote it down, and that was that. I heaved an enormous sigh of relief at not having to go down to the studio to face anyone with this lyric. Although Kern—and now Schwartz—had found it acceptable, I, by this time, was so mentally pooped that I felt it was just a collection of words adding up to very little. But, since it was over with, perhaps I could now get some sleep. (I realized some weeks later that I had come through, as requested, with a good, simple lyric—but if Schwartz hadn't told me of the imminent recording session I probably would have started on a fifth or sixth notion for the tune. Doubtless what had been throwing me was a feeling that the other *Cover Girl* lyrics were so much richer in rhyme and reference that they made this Miss Simplicity look like a wan wallflower.)

Dept. of You Never Can Tell, Who Knows?, That's Life, &c.: It turned out that this number was the biggest hit I'd had in any one year, with sheet-music sales of over six hundred thousand.

# HOW LONG
# HAS THIS BEEN GOING ON?

FUNNY FACE (1927). Music, George Gershwin. "Blues *moderato.*" Written for Adele Astaire and Jack Buchanan. Situation: a first kiss.

*He*

As a tot, when I trotted in little velvet
       panties,
I was kissed by my sisters, my cousins and
       my aunties.
Sad to tell, it was Hell—an Inferno worse
       than Dante's.
  So, my dear, I swore,
  "Never, nevermore!"
On my list I insisted that kissing must be
       crossed out.
Now I find I was blind, and, oh lady, how
       I've lost out!

*Refrain*

I could cry salty tears;
Where have I been all these years?
  Little wow,
  Tell me now:
How long has this been going on?

There were chills up my spine,
And some thrills I can't define.
  Listen, sweet,
  I repeat:
How long has this been going on?

277

Oh, I feel that I could melt;
  Into heaven I'm hurled—
I know how Columbus felt
  Finding another world.

Kiss me once, then once more.
What a dunce I was before!
    What a break—
    For heaven's sake!
How long has this been going on?

### *She*

'Neath the stars at bazaars often I've had to
                    caress men.
Five or ten dollars then I'd collect from all
                    those yes-men.
Don't be sad, I must add that they meant no more
                    than chessmen.
    Darling, can't you see
    'Twas for charity?
Though these lips have made slips, it was never
                    really serious.
Who'd 'a' thought I'd be brought to a state
                    that's so delirious?

### *Refrain*

I could cry salty tears;
Where have I been all these years?
    Listen, you—
    Tell me, do:
How long has this been going on?

What a kick—how I buzz!
Boy, you click as no one does!
    Hear me, sweet,
    I repeat:
How long has this been going on?

## The Element of Time

Dear, when in your arms I creep—
That divine rendezvous—
Don't wake me, if I'm asleep,
Let me dream that it's true.

Kiss me twice, then once more—
That makes thrice, let's make it four!
What a break—
For heaven's sake!
How long has this been going on?

---

*Blue Pencil Out of the Blue.* As if we didn't have enough on our minds in Philadelphia after *Funny Face* opened (cf. note to "Babbitt and Bromide"): I was at work in my room at the Ritz-Carlton when the telephone rang. The caller was the then professional manager of Shapiro Bernstein & Co., one of the three or four most important popular-music houses. He said: "I saw your show last night. Not very good." I agreed that we needed fixing. He: "You've got a number called 'How Long Has This Been Going On?' " Myself: "Yes, what about it?" He: "Doesn't mean a thing." I couldn't agree to that extent, but did concede its reception had been lukewarm; still, why his interest in this particular number? He: "Well, we bought a song with the same title and we're about to publish it. Yours is getting you nowhere, so how about taking it out of the show?"

This was as gratuitous a request as ever I heard. However, wanting little further insistence from him, I explained that eliminating a song from a book show wasn't a one-man job; that it would take some days before conferences reached the spot; that then, if decision called for elimination, a new song would have to be written, learned, staged, and orchestrated. So it was beyond me to help him out at the moment. I concluded by wishing him good luck on his song.

Well, he had *his* wish. A couple of weeks later on the road (either in Atlantic City or Washington) "How Long . . ." was out,

279

replaced by "He Loves and She Loves" (not as good a song as the former, but one that managed to get over). *My* wish (good luck), though, apparently didn't help, for even if the other "How Long . . ." was published, I've never heard it or of it.

\* \* \*

Two months later the eliminated song, because Ziegfeld liked it, found itself in *Rosalie*. There being no spot in the show for it as a duet, it became—with a few line changes—a solo for the soubrette, played by Bobbe Arnst.

# FOR YOU, FOR ME, FOR EVERMORE

THE SHOCKING MISS PILGRIM (1946). Music, George Gershwin. "Smoothly." Ballad duet for Dick Haymes and Betty Grable.

Paradise cannot refuse us—
Never such a happy pair!
Ev'rybody must excuse us
If we walk on air.
All the shadows now will lose us;
Lucky stars are ev'rywhere.
As a happy being,
Here's what I'm foreseeing:

*Refrain*

For you, for me, for evermore—
It's bound to be for evermore.
It's plain to see
We found, by finding each other,
The love we waited for.

I'm yours, you're mine, and in our hearts
The happy ending starts.
What a lovely world this world will be
With a world of love in store—
For you, for me, for evermore.

---

*Note for One Singer.* Possibly my lyric to this posthumous tune may be variation #4,708,903½, Series E, on the Three-Little-Words theme—but the song was considered good enough to be the principal ballad in *The Shocking Miss Pilgrim*. However, this is written neither to criticize nor to defend the words. The point: if a song is thought good enough and/or commercial enough or whatever enough to be recorded for public sale, why don't some singers check the lyric?

A recent album was called *For You, For Me, For Evermore,* so I bought it. The young lady who sang the title song had a pleasing voice, and the orchestral background, too, was good. But what happened to:

> What a lovely world this world will be
> With a world of love in store—
> For you, for me, for evermore

I cannot quite make the best of. She sings this as:

> What a lovely world this world *would* be
> With a *love that can endure*—
> For you, for me, for evermore.

Which changes tense and sense, and suddenly rhyme doesn't chime. On the album jacket the vocalist is quoted: "No, I don't read music . . . and all my own training was by ear." Good girl —but how about reading the words?

$$* \qquad * \qquad *$$

Once a musical composition is licensed to a recording organization, it becomes available for license to, and issuance by, any other company in the field. And, except for rare cases, neither publisher nor creators have any monitoring rights on the resultant performance. Still, even if given the privilege, it would be quite a job getting around to O.K.ing or N.G.ing songs like "Tea for Two," "Star Dust," "Night and Day," "Always," and others which become standards and eventually receive dozens, even hundreds, of recordings.

# LOVE IS HERE TO STAY

GOLDWYN FOLLIES (1938). Music, George Gershwin. *"Con anima."* Sung by Kenny Baker. Twelve years later, by Gene Kelly to Leslie Caron in MGM's *An American in Paris.*

The more I read the papers,
    The less I comprehend
The world and all its capers
    And how it all will end.
Nothing seems to be lasting,
    But that isn't our affair;
We've got something permanent—
    I mean, in the way we care.

*Refrain*

It's very clear
Our love is here to stay;
    Not for a year,
But ever and a day.

The radio and the telephone
And the movies that we know
May just be passing fancies—
And in time may go.

    But oh, my dear,
Our love is here to stay.
    Together we're
Going a long, long way.

In time the Rockies may crumble,
Gibraltar may tumble
(They're only made of clay),
But—our love is here to stay.

So little footage was given to "Love Is Here to Stay"—I think only one refrain—that it meant little in *The Goldwyn Follies*. Beautifully presented in the Academy Award-winning musical *An American in Paris,* it became better known.

When George and I were on the *Goldwyn Follies* we managed to finish five songs the first six weeks of our contract. (Vernon Duke and I fixed up a couple of missing verses later.) The five were: "I Love to Rhyme," "Love Walked In," "I Was Doing All Right," "Just Another Rhumba" (the longest and most ambitious, but not used), and "Love Is Here to Stay." The reason we worked this fast on the vocal contributions was to allow the composer to have the following six or eight weeks free to write a ballet for Zorina. As it turned out, our first six weeks were George's last six weeks of work; and "Love Is Here to Stay" the last song he composed.

# Turns with Terpsichore

*"Shall We Dance?"*

*"Shoes with Wings On"*

*"In Three-Quarter Time"*

*"I Can't Be Bothered Now"*

*"Stairway to Paradise"*

# SHALL WE DANCE?

SHALL WE DANCE (1937). Music, George Gershwin. "Brightly and rhythmically." Sung by Fred Astaire.

> Drop that long face! Come on, have your fling!
>   Why keep nursing the blues?
> If you want this old world on a string,
>   Put on your dancing shoes—
>     Stop wasting time!
>   Put on your dancing shoes—
>     Watch your spirits climb.

> *Refrain*
>
> Shall we dance, or keep on moping?
> Shall we dance, and walk on air?
> Shall we give in to despair—
> Or shall we dance with never a care?
>
> Life is short; we're growing older.
>   Don't you be an also-ran.
> You'd better dance, little lady!
>   Dance, little man!
>   Dance whenever you can!

---

This simple lyric reads as though it might be an exercise in Basic English; certainly not an emanation of the "time's a-fleeting" boys from Horace to Herrick. But the distinctive tune it was fitted to brings to the listener (me, anyway) an overtone of moody and urgent solicitude.

\*     \*     \*

*The Lady from Montana.* When *Stepping Toes,* the original name for the script we were working from, was changed to *Shall We Dance,* the producer asked for a title song, and this one resulted. Five or six weeks later we were still at work at RKO when the legal department telephoned that there was trouble: a woman in Montana threatened to sue because she had written a waltz called "Shall We Dance," which hadn't been published but had been played once on a radio station in Butte. Legal departments of the studios worry a great deal—the film industry being particularly vulnerable to, and apprehensive of, nuisance litigation—so we got in touch with our publisher's lawyer in New York. Investigation through the Copyright Office showed registration over the years of at least half a dozen songs called "Shall We Dance." That fact did not stop the RKO legal department's headshaking; they continued to worry.

I never did find out who worked it out, or how; but do recall that the settlement was a charming one: RKO would permit the publication of the Montanan "Shall We Dance" if its composer could find a publisher; also, on her next visit to her married daughter in Los Angeles, the studio would see that she got two admissions to any theater showing the film at the time.

# SHOES WITH WINGS ON

THE BARKLEYS OF BROADWAY (1949). Music, Harry
Warren. "With a good beat." The vocal section of Fred Astaire's
one-man ballet in a shoe shop.

Aladdin had a wonderful lamp,
King Midas had the touch of gold;
In magic they had many a champ
'Way back in days of old.
But magic was in its infancy;
Today they'd ring no bell.
Today they'd mimic
Me and my gimmick
To cast a spell.

*Refrain*

When I've got shoes with wings on—
The Winter's gone, the Spring's on.
When I've got shoes with wings on—
The town is full of rhythm and the world's in rhyme.

The Neon City glows up;
My pretty Pretty shows up.
We'll dance until they close up—
(Got my Guardian Angel working overtime.)

I give Aladdin the lamp,
Midas the gold.
Who needs a wizard or magician
In the old tradition?
That's not competition—
I've got 'em beat a thousandfold!
Why?

'Cause I've got shoes with wings on—
And living has no strings on.
I put those magic things on,
   And I go flying with 'em—
   And the town is full of rhythm
   And the world's in rhyme.

---

It's tough to get a title for a song about a dance. By which rhythmic remark I mean that unless you're bent on inventing a new stage or ballroom frisk to be called "Do the Hoopla Poopla" or "The Whatchamacallit Ha Cha Cha," you're usually limited to titles like "Dancing Shoes" or "May I Have the Next Dance, Please, Madame?" and such. So, when looking up something else in Bulfinch a picture of Mercury with his winged cap and winged sandals brought the notion of "Shoes with Wings On" for an Astaire solo, I thought: "Well, even if just the least bit, it's at least a little bit different for a dance title." But leaden rather than mercurial were the time and effort spent on the lyric to fit Warren's tricky tune. There was much juggling and switching and throwing out of line and phrase and rhyme—maybe ten days' worth—before the words made some singable sort of sense. Wodehouse once told me that the greatest challenge (and greatest worry) to him in lyric-writing was to come across a section of a tune requiring three double rhymes. And I well realized what this special torture was when I tackled "wings on." When I finally wound up with "wings on—strings on—things on," that was *that,* and I felt like a suddenly unburdened Atlas.

# IN THREE-QUARTER TIME*

PARDON MY ENGLISH (1933). Music, George Gershwin.
Opening by Ensemble. Act I. A beer garden in Dresden.

When Fred'rick the Great was at Potsdam
  The French introduced the gavotte;
    But Fred warned his henchmen
    'Twas all right for Frenchmen—
  But Germans? But certainly not!
"With waltzes we'll build up the Empire;
  For waltzes," said Freddy, "I fight!"
    So poet and peasant
    From then to the present
  Have waltzed all the day and the night.
If a *Musiker* doesn't bring Strauss mit 'im,
He is no *Musiker*—'raus mit 'im!

### *Refrain*

We laugh and we sing, Oom-pah-pah,
  And we dance—in three-quarter time.
When having our fling, Oom-pah-pah,
  We romance—in three-quarter time.
    'Way back in German hist'ry
    When Man began to climb,
      We're certain that Adam
      Made love to his madam
    In three-quarter time,
        So—
    *Me* for *three*-four time.

*Second Half of Second Refrain*

From Dusseldorf to Frankfurt,
  From Lentz to Schnableheim,
    The petticoat gender
    Will always surrender
  To three-quarter time,
          So—
    *Me* for *three*-four,
    *Pooh* for *two*-four,
    *Me* for *three*-four time!

---

With new words, the music of the verse was reprised somewhere in Act II to introduce short specialty dances. Thus this oversimplified generalization about dance tempi:

The way we respond to the ¾,
  We're Germans, you tell at a glance;
    Identification
    Of many a nation
  Is tied up with tempo in dance.
The Irishman's fond of the ⁶⁄₈;
  For ³⁄₈ the Spaniard goes mad.
    The Yankee goes more for
    The ha-cha-cha ⁴⁄₄;
  With ⁵⁄₄ the Russian is had.
And to make the point comprehensible,
A few steps are now indispensable.
          (*business of various dances*)

# I CAN'T BE BOTHERED NOW

A DAMSEL IN DISTRESS (1937). Music, George Gershwin. "Well marked." Jerry Halliday (Fred Astaire), celebrated American performer, entertains a London theater queue.

Music is the magic makes a gloomy day sunshiny;
Dance to it and troubles all seem tiny.
When I'm dancing I don't care if this old world stops
    turning,
Or if my bank is burning—
Or even if Roumania
Wants to fight Albania. . . .

*Refrain*

Bad news, go 'way!
Call 'round some day
In March or May—
I can't be bothered now.

My bonds and shares
May fall downstairs—
Who cares, who cares?
I'm dancing and I can't be bothered now.

I'm up among the stars;
On earthly things I frown.
I'm throwing off the bars
That held me down.

I'll pay the piper
When times are riper.
Just now I shan't—
Because you see I'm dancing and I can't——
Be bothered now.

---

Memory doesn't serve me on this one, so you won't be bothered now with anything on its coming-to-be. My only recollection is a not too surprising one: Fred Astaire performed it superbly.

# (I'LL BUILD A)
# STAIRWAY TO PARADISE

GEORGE WHITE'S SCANDALS, "Fourth Annual Production" (1922). "Words by B. G. De Sylva and Arthur Francis" (the latter a pseudonym for I.G.). Music, George Gershwin. Finale Act I: "The Patent Leather Forest." Sung by all principals, including Producer George White; also on stage, Paul Whiteman and the Palais Royal Orchestra.

> All you preachers
> Who delight in panning the dancing teachers,
> Let me tell you there are a lot of features
> Of the dance that carry you through
> The Gates of Heaven.
>
> It's madness
> To be always sitting around in sadness,
> When you could be learning the Steps of Gladness.
> (You'll be happy when you can do
> Just six or seven.)
>
> Begin today. You'll find it nice:
> The quickest way to Paradise.
> When you practice,
> Here's the thing to know—
> Simply say as you go:
>
> *Refrain* (*Con spirito*)
>
> I'll build a Stairway to Paradise,
>   With a new Step ev'ry day.
> I'm going to get there at any price;
>   Stand aside, I'm on my way!

## Turns with Terpsichore

> I got the blues
> And up above it's so fair;
> Shoes,
> Go on and carry me there!
> I'll build a Stairway to Paradise
> With a new Step ev'ry day.

---

One day lyricist B. G. (Buddy) De Sylva said to me: "I've been thinking about a song you and George wrote, that 'New Step Every Day.' Anything particular in mind for it?" I said No—it was just a song, and not much of one. He then told me: "I think the last line has an idea for a production number. If you like, we could write it up and I *think* it could be used in the *Scandals*."

(The verse of "A New Step Every Day" began:

> I can dance the old gavotte,
> I can shimmy, I can trot, &c.,

and the refrain dwelt on the euphoric effect of various dances and the desire to learn new ones, winding up with:

> I'll build a staircase to Paradise,
> With a new step ev'ry day.)

Naturally I was tickled to be able to collaborate on something for the *Scandals*. The next night George and I had dinner in De Sylva's Greenwich Village apartment, and about nine p.m. we started on the new song. About two a.m. it was completed, verse included. Outside of the line De Sylva liked, the result was totally different from the simple ditty "A New Step Every Day"—and even "staircase" had become "stairway." The new song had a complicated, for those days, twenty-four-bar verse, replete with sixteenth notes and thick chords, plus a refrain with key changes. I agreed with Buddy and George that it sounded like a good first-act production-finale, but figured my returns would be program credit and nothing else; the song seemed too difficult for popular publication.

Honestly surprised to learn just before the out-of-town opening that the song was to be one of the show's seven published numbers, I was pleased—but who would buy it? Especially as the boys had written an out-and-out commercial song they weren't too proud of: "I Found a Four Leaf Clover (And the Next Day I Found You)"—an obvious concession to the popular ear, a song with so pronounced a Sousa march quality and the soldiers' "Tipperary"-like beat that it inevitably must sweep the country. (My father, when referring to it, kept saying: "Play me that war song.")

Well, I was wrong. The bands around town and some record companies played up "Stairway to Paradise" more than anything else in the show, and it became a hit—that is, for a revue. (Most hit songs from the stage emerge from musicals rather than revues.) "Four Leaf Clover" attracted little attention, while my one third of "Stairway's" royalties amounted to thirty-five hundred dollars, enough to support me for a year.

\*　　　\*　　　\*

I forgot to mention that there was a patter attached to "Stairway," which we added some days later. It was a week's Dance Diet; here are a couple of the prescriptions:

> On Monday—happy as a lark
> You'll be getting started when you learn to Toe the Mark.
> (*Demonstrate step*) That's the Toe the Mark.
> On Wednesday—walk around the block
> And at every corner do the Eagle Rock.
> (*Demonstrate step*) That's the Eagle Rock. &c.

\*　　　\*　　　\*

P.S. Even though a newly revised rhyming dictionary (Burgess Johnson's) lists "feature" with "teacher," I doubt that I'd rhyme them today.

# The State of the Union

*"In Our United State"*

*"Love Is Sweeping the Country"*

*"A Kiss for Cinderella"*

*"The Land of Opportunitee"*

# IN OUR UNITED STATE

GIVE A GIRL A BREAK (1953). Music, Burton Lane. "Moderately." Nighttime in Manhattan. Boy and Girl out for a stroll see the lighted windows in the distant UN Building, where evidently an important night session is in progress. Sung by Debbie Reynolds and Bob Fosse.

The state of the world is such
That the world is in quite a state.
But let's not worry too much;
Let the rest of the world debate.
Right now the thing to discuss
Is the wonderful status of us.

*Refrain*

The state of our union,
Hearts in communion,
Never will know any foreign entanglements;
Outsiders will not rate
In our united state!

We'll make the altar
Strong as Gibraltar—
Fooling around will be unconstitutional.
Great will be our united state!

With nothing but true love in the ascendance,
We'll always sign and renew
A Declaration of Dependence—
Where you depend on me
And I depend on you.

Peaceful and cozy,
We'll have a rosy
Future with a House of cute Representatives;
So, I can hardly wait,
Darling, for our united state!

### Second Refrain

Our annual budget?
I'll let you judge it—
You do what you will with what's in our treasury;
I won't investigate
In our united state.

This is my platform:
That face and that form!
You will find that that's a permanent policy
Slated for our united state.

But there will be changes I'll be unfolding:
Withholding taxes are through—
For when it's you, dear, that I'm holding,
You can't withhold on me—
I can't withhold on you.

We'll have a White House,
Small, but a bright house,
Built on the Pursuit of Star-Spangled Happiness.
Hurry, let's name the date,
Darling, for our united state!

---

*Technical Note.* In the refrain the third lines in stanzas A, B, and D end in dactyls, a set-up which could call for a trio of triple rhymes. But "foreign entanglements," "unconstitutional," and "Representatives" are words importantly germane to the theme; also, with the rest of the refrain closely rhymed—e.g., *"Great*

will be our united *state*"—they give an unexpected tickle to the
ear; they may dangle but do not jangle (I think). Too, even if
triple rhymes were arrived at, they'd be lost in the shuffle, since
the lines they'd belong to are so far apart. (If this isn't clear, skip
it; the song sold less than a hundred copies.)

*Reading a Lyric without Benefit of the Tune.* One who reads
the verse of this song without knowing the melody, will accent certain words thus:

> The *state* of the *world* is *such*
> That the *world* is in *quite* a *state,* &c.

and one will, as the quiz-masters have it, be absolutely correct.
Correct because the music here happens to accent the same words.

But when it comes to the refrain, the reader isn't aware that the
unknown melody has emphasized unexpected syllables and words.
For instance, the reading will probably be:

> Out-*side*-rs will not rate
> In *our* united state.

And

> I *won't* investigate
> In *our* united state.

Whereas one learns, when hearing the song sung, that the melody
has shifted the accents to stress:

> *Out*-siders will not rate
> *In* our united state.

And, in the same fashion, "I" and "In" are on notes getting the
downbeat—not "won't" and "our." Sidney Lanier (1842–1881)
and others have written formidable books given mostly to the thesis
that the laws governing music and verse are identical; but, say
what you will (even—it shouldn't happen to a doggerel), where
*song* is involved, music frequently makes for prosodic perversion—
and no contest. This is why some songwriters, when demonstrating
a new song to a publisher or some possible performer, do not

bother with exact punctuation in the typewritten lyric they hand the listener; they merely use capital letters throughout.

Thus an old-time lyricist might or might not today submit:

> WHO IS SYLVIA WHAT IS SHE
> THAT ALL OUR SWAINS COMMEND HER
> HOLY FAIR AND WISE IS SHE
> THE HEAVEN SUCH GRACE DID LEND HER
> THAT SHE MIGHT ADMIRED BE, &c.

# LOVE IS SWEEPING THE COUNTRY

OF THEE I SING (1931). Music, George Gershwin. John P. Wintergreen runs for President on a platform with a single plank: Love. This campaign workers' song rousingly sung outside Madison Square Garden by George Murphy and June O'Dea.

> Why are people gay
> All the night and day,
> Feeling as they never felt before?
> What is the thing
> That makes them sing?

> Rich man, poor man, thief,
> Doctor, lawyer, chief
> Feel a feeling that they can't ignore;
> It plays a part
> In ev'ry heart,
> And ev'ry heart is shouting "Encore!"

> *Refrain*

> Love is sweeping the country;
> Waves are hugging the shore;
> All the sexes
> From Maine to Texas
> Have never known such love before.

> See them billing and cooing
> Like the birdies above!
> Girl and boy alike,
> Sharing joy alike,
> Feel that passion'll
> Soon be national.
> Love is sweeping the country—
> There never was so much love!

*Patter*

Spring is in the air—
    Each mortal loves his neighbor;
Who's that loving pair?
    That's Capital and Labor.

Florida and Cal-
    Ifornia get together
In a festi*val*
    Of oranges and weather.

Boston upper zones
    Are changing social habits,
And I hear the Cohns
    Are taking up the Cabots.

Cities are above
    The quarrels that were hapless.
Look who's making love:
    St. Paul and Minneap'lis!

---

Shortly after this song was completed I thought it could stand a patter. George reflected a moment, then: "Let's use the patter music from the *East Is West* opening." (We'd written a quite elaborate opening for that unproduced opus. At one stage in it, just before the Love Boat arrived with its bevy of Sing-Song Girls to be auctioned off, a quartet of mandarins sang their preferences.) And that's why the music to the present patter, slightly changed from the original, sounds a touch Chinese.

Although mandarins were supposedly highly educated, it seems that I slanged up their Mandarin a bit. Here are a couple of the qualifications required of the girls on the block.

304

## The State of the Union

### One Mandarin

I come here to seek
   A high-tone baby, *Class* A;
Beautiful and chic,
   And up-to-date, not *pass*-é.

### Another

No say "Oh, you kid!"
   To any thin or flat one;
I am here to bid—
   But only for a fat one.

# A KISS FOR CINDERELLA

OF THEE I SING (1931). Music, George Gershwin. Part of Finale, Act I. Steps of the Capitol, Washington, D.C. The Supreme Court is present to supervise John P. Wintergreen's inauguration as President and his marriage to Mary Turner. Other dignitaries and guests are also in attendance. William Gaxton as Wintergreen.

*Ensemble ("grandioso")*

Hail! Hail! The ruler of our gov'ment!
Hail! Hail! The man who taught what love meant!
    Clear, clear the way
    For his inaugural and wedding day.
            *(Wintergreen and Mary appear.)*

*Wintergreen*

I have definite ideas about the deficit;
I have plans about our tonnage on the ocean.
But before I grow statistical I'll preface it
With a statement growing out of pure emotion;
    For on this glorious day I find
    I'm sentimentally inclined,
        And so—
I sing this to the girls I used to know:
    *(and he goes into the Bachelor's Farewell Routine.)*

A KISS FOR CINDERELLA *(gracefully)*

Here's a kiss for Cinderella
    And a parting kiss for May,
    Toodle-oo, goodbye, this is my wedding day.

Here's a parting smile for Della
    And the lady known as Lou.
    Toodle-oo, goodbye, with bach'lor days I'm through!

# The State of the Union

Tho' I really never knew them,
　　It's a rule I must obey;
So I'm saying goodbye to them
　　In the customary way.

My regards to Arabella
　　And to Emmaline and Kay!
　　Toodle-oo, dear girls, goodbye!
　　This is my wedding day.

(*He repeats the refrain, as girls come down to footlights and, in a counter-melody, explain to audience:*)

He is toodle-ooing all his lady loves,
　　All the girls he didn't know so well,
All the innocent and all the shady loves,
　　Oh, ding-a-dong-a-dell!
Bride and groom, their future should be glorious,
　　What a happy story they will tell;
Let the welkin now become uproarious,
　　Oh, ding-a-dong-a-dell!

### Ensemble

Hail! Hail! The mighty ruler of love!
Hail! Hail! The man who made us love love!
　　Hip! hip! hurray!
　　For his inaugural and wedding day!

---

This one fits its category doubly: Wintergreen and Mary Turner are united not only for better or worse, but the State of the Union is again represented by their becoming, in the one ceremony, Chief Executive and First Lady of the Union.

The main portion of this section—"A Kiss for Cinderella" and its counter-melody—is a take-off on the bachelor-farewell type of song, best exemplified by John Golden and Ivan Caryll's "Goodbye, Girls, I'm Through" (*Chin-Chin,* 1914).

\*　　\*　　\*

For the four-line Inaugural Speech I have here used the version written for the 1952 *Of Thee I Sing* revival. The original four lines as sung (and printed in the vocal score) are:

> I have definite ideas about the Philippines,
> And the herring situation up in Bismarck;
> I have notions on the salaries of movie queens,
> And the men who sign their signatures with *this* mark.
>
>          (*He makes an X in the air.*)

Although "Bismarck" and "this mark" make a good rhyme and give the performer the business of making a signature cross, I probably felt that a mild joke based on Bismarck herring wasn't good enough for the show which twenty years earlier had won the Pulitzer Prize.

# THE LAND OF OPPORTUNITEE

PARK AVENUE (1946). Music, Arthur Schwartz. A calypso about the stock market, the race track, and quiz programs. Sung in Trinidadian rhythms and dialect by four dinner-jacketed, well-heeled Park Avenue gentlemen. *N.B.:* No phonetic spelling is attempted. Many vowels, though, vary in their vocal values. Thus, "land" should be pronounced *"lond"*; "immigrants," *"immigrahnts"*; "told," *"tulled"*; "gold," *"gulled"*; "man," *"mahn,"* &c.

### Introduction

All the immigrants came to the U.S.A.
   Because they had been told
That in ev'ry cit*ee* of the U.S.A.
   The streets were paved with gold.

They dug themselves a pile,
Then went back to Italy and the Emerald Isle.

In the U.S.A. not all the gold is gone—
The pioneer spirit still carry on.
   For example and to wit—
   We give you a sample of it:

### 1

You take the subway to the street called Wall;
On a dignified broker's man you call.
He shows you a ticker goes tick, tick, tick—
And helps you a stock to pick, pick, pick.

Fascinating names you have from which to choose,
Biggest corporations which cannot lose:

Delaware and Lackawanna,
United Fruit and Banana—
Or you buy Nash Kelvinator,
Maybe Otis Elevator.
  Oh boy, can't miss!
Anaconda Copper Mining,
'Merican Smelting and Refining;
Biggest bargains ever wuz,
Like Paramount and Warner Bros.
  Oh boy, some class!

With a thousand corporations to pick from—
You clean up, my friend, or else you're dumb.

### Refrain

You buy a block of stock, say, American Tel;
Goes up a hundred points, then quickly you sell.
  Making a fortune is A B C,
  In the Grand Land of Opportunitee.

### 2

By now you have piled up such a bundle of jack
You take a taxi to the nearest race track.
Is easy to take the race track by storm—
A pencil, a program, a "Racing Form."

Then you handicap the possibilities
By the Past Performances of all the gee-gees:

Man-o'-War, Sun Beau and Stymie—
.They have not done badly by me.
Good-bye, Care!—and also, Trouble!
(Compliments of Daily Double)
  Oh boy, some tips!
In the first, I like Disraeli;
In the second race, Rose Bailey.
In the big race, Tom the Peeper—
(Looks to me like he's a sleeper.)
  Oh boy, sure things!

## The State of the Union

So you study and study all the dope you got,
And at the window you bet a long *shot*.

*Refrain*

They're at the gate—and off! The race she is run.
Your horse comes in and pays a 100 to 1.
    Making a fortune is A B C,
    In the Grand Land of Opportunitee.

### 3

Though now you have got of money quite a store,
After all you're only human, so you want more.
So you go to a radio show which is
A question and answer program known as quiz.

When you face the mike you make no faux-pas;
All night long you studied the Britannica:

        What's the color of red roses?
        On your feet how many toes is?
        Name the month after September.
        What's on 25th December?
            Oh boy, oh boy!
        In one day how many hours?
        Oranges are fruits or flowers?
        Which is more, ten or eleven?
        Just what year was Nineteen-Seven?
            Oh boy, quiz kid!

Your answers have put the man in his place,
But now the big moment you must face.

*Refrain*

The questioner he ask you, "What is your name?"
You get a $100,000 if you tell him the same.
  Making a fortune is A B C,
  In the Grand Land of Opportunitee.
    And—
If you know what flag is Red, White and Blue,
He will throw in the sponsor's daughter too.
  Making a fortune is A B C,
  In the Grand Land of Opportunitee.

*Tag*

Is so simple, anyone can do it.
  You just open an account . . .
  Take a taxi to the track . . .
  Give the answers on a quiz . . .
Nothing to it!

---

Although calypso music generally hasn't as much variety in rhythm and melody as has, say, Brazilian popular song, no song form anywhere is more all-inclusive in subject matter than the Trinidadian. The improvised calypso, with its odd syllabic stress and loose rhyme, can narrate, advise, philosophize, fulminate, use this morning's headlines—and any theme goes, including the political and sexual. Thanks to subject matter and Schwartz's varied rhythms, our longish "Land of Opportunitee" sat well with the audience.

\*  \*  \*

I didn't have to do much research on this song's subject matter. Remembered experiences and experiments were enough. For instance:

*Subject Matter A:* The Stock Market

In the fall of 1919 I learned of two ex-classmates who pooled $150 apiece, went to Wall Street and, on a ten-per-cent margin, doubled their money in a few days. I couldn't resist joining them in downtown Midas Land, so drew out the $160 I had in a savings bank, sold a $50 Liberty Bond (the net savings of a four-month tour with a carnival earlier that year), and opened a checking account at the State Bank a few blocks from my home. When I told my father I was going down to Wall Street, where my classmates were making a fortune, he said: "You'll make so much money you'll go broke." Then, as an afterthought: "By the way, I don't know anything about stocks, but at the pinochle club last night I remember them talking about Sinclair Oil something—Sinclair Oil 'rights,' I think they said."

Next morning about 10:30 I got to Clark and Hubbard's, a small Curb house. After being welcomed by my classmates—there were now half a dozen—I was asked by the firm's cashier if I had anything in mind. Informed of my interest in Sinclair Oil rights, he stuck his head into the private office and had a quote yelled back at him; the rights were selling at ⅛ or 12½ cents each. When I mentioned how much money was available, he said: "Well, you can get yourself a thousand rights for $125, plus $6 in commissions. You'll have to pay cash, though, as it's too small a transaction to be margined." That was O.K. A few minutes later I made out a check for $131; and I was now the fully paid owner of a thousand Sinclair Oil rights—whatever they were. (Afterwards I learned that they gave the holder the right to buy newly issued Sinclair stock at $60 a share.)

At noon I joined the boys for lunch at Child's. Over coffee and Danish pastry, the world economic situation was discussed: would the coal strike in England affect such-and-such a stock? how important to the market was the rebel uprising in Bolivia?—and other matters of financial moment. Later, back again at the customers' room, I was reminiscing with the boys when, about 2:30, the cashier tapped me on the shoulder and said: "You'd better do something about those rights before three o'clock." "What happened?" I asked. "Well, I'm sure you know they expire today, and they're no good after the closing." I *didn't* know, and said: "What do I do?" He shrugged. "Sell at the market, of course." So I sold at the market. And in a few minutes came the announcement: "Sold a thousand Sinclair rights at $\frac{1}{64}$." Which sale, minus commissions, netted me some $12. (This speedy dwindling of my capital taught me a valuable lesson: don't invest in rights to buy new shares at $60 when outstanding shares are selling at 59½. Especially don't on the day the rights expire.)

My first misadventure didn't discourage me. Next day I went partners with a classmate—each putting up $50 for margin—on ten shares of a railway stock selling at 98. Nothing much happened. So, after three or four days, I persuaded my partner that we should sell. We broke about even. Fine with me. When I arrived at the office next morning, however, I got a dirty look from my ex-partner. After the previous day's closing the Supreme Court had made some decision favorable to the railroad, and the stock had opened at 108 and was heading higher. Overnight we could have more than doubled our margin money. After one or two more unprofitable deals I quit my career as a market plunger.

In the late Twenties, with several successful shows under my belt, I was able to enter the market on a somewhat larger scale, and kept on adding my royalties to, eventually, three margin accounts. Needless to say, all three were wiped out in the '29 crash. And in '31, again on margin, I lost my *Delicious* Hollywood earnings. But I have always believed in common stocks, and since I began to buy them outright some ten or fifteen years ago I have more than made up my earlier losses.

✳　　✳　　✳

### Subject Matter B: THE RACE TRACK

When a meet is on in town I try to get out at least on Saturdays. Like most visitors to the mutuel machine, I lose. But I enjoy the races and whimsical betting. At Hollywood Park once I bet on all twelve horses in a race and won a few dollars when $2 on a long shot paid over $50. On the other hand—and more typical—I bet on seven horses in an eleven-horse race, mostly $2 each and $2 across on a couple. What both amused and bemused me was not that I didn't win, but that my horses ran fifth to eleventh—I didn't even get fourth. However, it isn't entirely true, as my friends claim, that I am a completely unlucky player. I once won on

# The State of the Union

On a Friday night in the first week of May 1940 I boarded the crack train, the City of Los Angeles, on my way to New York to begin work on *Lady in the Dark*. After breakfast the next morning I was in the club car, reading. There was little conviviality among the passengers because France had just been invaded by Germany and the world looked a mess. But, mess or not, some sort of business was going on here, as I saw the steward addressing the individual passengers. When he came to my seat I learned a pool had been started on that afternoon's Kentucky Derby—and would I care to invest $5 in it? I gave him the money and sometime later he came around with a hat containing paper slips and asked me to draw one. The slip I pulled was "Gallahadion." This was a horse I had seen at Santa Anita, where he had won a race or two, but I knew the sports pages considered him a rank outsider in the Derby. Good-bye $5, but in a worth-while cause.

Just before dinner I asked the steward who had won the race, and he told me that, although many of the passengers had radios with window aerials, no one had been able to receive the results, as we were in mountain country. Sunday morning I got off the train at one of the stops and bought a copy of the *Rocky Mountain News*, but it carried no Derby information. Late that afternoon I was in my compartment when there was a knock at the door and the steward appeared. "Congratulations, Mr. Gershwin. Gallahadion won." "Really? What did he pay?" "I don't know exactly, but he was about 35 to 1." My long shot and ship had come in.

"Congratulations again, and here you are, sir," and he handed me a rather smallish envelope. I opened it and found three $5 bills in it. He saw my look of puzzlement and explained: "There were seven players—that's $35. $5 came off the top for handling the pool, leaving $30. The winner gets $15, the second horse $10, the third $5." "I see," I said. "Here's $5 for yourself." And that's how I won the Kentucky Derby, winding up with even money on a 35-to-1 shot.

*       *       *

315

### Subject Matter C: Quiz Programs

Impressed by my workroom's collection of dictionaries, encyclopedias, atlases, and other books of reference, some visitors think I ought to be a wiz at crossword puzzles, double-crostics, scrabble, and other word games. But I'm not. Memory serves me better recalling personal experiences and incidents than knowing what high offices three Romans, each named Marcus Aemillius Lepidus, held. (I came across them ten minutes ago and have already forgotten.) So personal question-and-answer experiences are out of the question.

All I can tell here is that when "Opportunitee" was written, the most popular quiz program was "Take It or Leave It" ("The $64 Question"); and when I wrote "You get $100,000 . . ." that figure was in the realm of sheer fantasy. Today, though, that then incredible amount seems to be chickenfeed compared to sums awarded contestants in the past few years.

# A Miscellany of Acclaim

*"A Rhyme for Angela"*

*"The Lorelei"*

*"Tributes to Liza Elliott"*

*"The Illegitimate Daughter"*

*"Alessandro the Wise"*

*"Wintergreen for President"*

# A RHYME FOR ANGELA

THE FIREBRAND OF FLORENCE (1945). Music, Kurt
Weill. "Lively and graceful." Library of the Palazzo. Duke Alessandro, never having failed to win a coveted maid by lyricizing
her, attempts again the tactic, this time hoping to intrigue Cellini's
model, Angela. He tries his poetic effort out on a group of Ladies-
in-Waiting, who listen well but, more entertainingly, dance with
him after the second refrain. Sung by Melville Cooper.

It's always been a pleasure
To dedicate a measure
To the lady who intrigues me at the time.
Diana and Roxana
And Lana and Susannah
Were names I sang in rhythm and in rhyme.
Cornelia and Aurelia,
Cecelia and Ophelia
Inspired lovely lyrics from my pen—
But Angela is something else again.

*Refrain*

I can find a rhyme for Lucy—
For instance, her kiss is juicy.
But I must confess
I'm lost, more or less,
With Angela, Angela.

Takes no time to rhyme, say, Chloe—
For instance, her breast is snowy.
But rhyming is lame
When you get a name
Like Angela, Angela.

319

If only they called her Olivia,
She could be a cute bit of trivia;
   If she were tagged Maria,
   Or even Dorothea,
   She'd be my Sole Mia
      Divine.

I can find a rhyme for Irma:
She's Heaven on Terra Firma.
   But Angela has no patter—
   And yet, what does it matter
   If Angela's heart rhymes with mine!

*Second Refrain*

I can find a rhyme for Margot:
On her favors there's no embargo.
   But rhyming is tough
   When one's bit of fluff
      Is Angela, Angela.

What a joy to rhyme Amanda:
Each movement is pure propaganda.
   (The heights I can climb—
   Till I seek a rhyme
      For Angela, Angela.)

If only her name were Titania,
I'd star her in my miscellanea;
   If she were called Marcella
   Or even Isabella
   This most poetic fella
      Could shine.

I can find a rhyme for Edith:
She possesses what Everyman needeth.
   But Angela has no patter—
   And yet, what does it matter
   If Angela's heart rhymes with mine!

Rhyming feminine given names presents little difficulty, there being so many to choose from. (Withycombe's interesting *The Oxford Dictionary of English Christian Names* lists about six hundred female; and many new ones, I'm sure, continue to be bestowed at christenings by imaginative and/or reckless parents.) Had "Angela" required an encore, these were some of the left-overs:

> If only her name were Mercedes,
> She'd bring me both Heaven and Hades.

> Among other graces, Hermione
> Would feature an ankle that's ti-o-ny.

> (fill in) ................ Amy,
> I'm jelly when her eyes survey me.

> (fill in) ................ Cora,
> A lovely from Sodom and Gomorrah.

> (fill in) ................ Charlotte,
> A mixture of angel and harlot.

&c., &c.

\*     \*     \*

*Rhyme and Time.* It was fitting that Alessandro try his hand at rhyming, as by his time the Italians had been making use of this verbal or syllabic harmonization for some centuries. (Petrarch declared the Italians learned the device from the Sicilians; the Sicilians stated they acquired it from the Provençals; the Provençals felt they'd inherited the chiming effect from their erstwhile masters, the Arabians, while the Germans maintained they had adopted it from the Scandinavians. And so on.)

In his *Amenities of Literature,* erudite Isaac D'Israeli (father of brilliant "Dizzy") has an essay on the origin of rhyme and is rather severe with those antiquarians who believe that the invention of rhyme arose among the above-mentioned European peoples. He backs up only the scholars who state that rhyme was known to, and practiced by, the ancients, especially "in the Hebrew, in the Sanscrit, . . . and in the Chinese poetry. . . ." (He is not quite that certain about the Greeks and the Romans.) He concludes: "We might as well inquire the origin of dancing as that of rhyming: the rudest society as well as the most polished practiced these arts at every era. And thus it has happened . . . that the origin of rhyme was everywhere sought for, and everywhere found."

Some authorities today still state that rhyme was known and used by the ancients (always excluding the Greeks and the Romans). But most of the articles I've looked up feel that exact rhyme came into use in late Latin about the third century A.D. when, in the Catholic Church ritual, priests of the African Coptic Church found it not only pleasing to the ear but also a mnemonic aid.

\*     \*     \*

*Rhyme and "Time."* To give the correct pronunciation of proper nouns, the popular newsweekly *Time* has for many years used the phrase "rhymes with." Thus, for example: "Donizetti (rhymes with jetty)" or "Truman (rhymes with human)," &c.—and O.K. But in many other instances, "rhymes with" shouldn't appear, for when one reads "Orwell (rhymes with doorbell)" or "Longstreet (rhymes with wrong beat)," &c., these aren't being rhymed correctly. What is being done is that *Time* is rhyming each syllable perpendicularly instead of double-rhyming the name horizontally.

\*     \*     \*

*A Short Refresher Course.* In double, or triple, or rhymes of more than three syllables, one rhymes *only* the accented syllable, and the syllables that follow must be identical in sound. For instance: (double) LONG street, WRONG street; JIFfy, IF he; (triple) vaRIety, improPRIety; VAcancy, THEY can see; (quadruple) LYRically, saTIRically; MORE if I love, GLORify love.

322

From the second set of rhymes in each example one will notice that spelling is not a determinant in rhyme, since (again): rhyme is based solely on the pronunciation and harmonization of accented syllables.

(Most modern poets find "perfect" or "full" or "exact" rhyme too limiting, and favor sound devices called "visual rhyme," "suspended rhyme," "historical rhyme," "dissonance-consonance," and other literary and intellectual varieties. These are not, I feel, for the lyricist, whose output in the field of entertainment must be easily assimilable and whose work depends a good deal on perfect rhyme's jingle.)

# THE LORELEI

PARDON MY ENGLISH (1933). Music, George Gershwin. *"Moderato."* Setting: a beer garden in Dresden. Sung by Lyda Roberti on the road; then, because of book changes and song switches, by the team of Randall and Newberry.

Back in the days of knights in armor
There once lived a lovely charmer;
 Swimming in the Rhine
 Her figure was divine.
She had a yen for all the sailors:
Fishermen and gobs and whalers.
 She had a most immoral eye;
 They called her Lorelei.
 She created quite a stir—
 And I want to be like her.

*Refrain*

I want to be like that gal on the river
 Who sang her songs to the ships passing by;
She had the goods and how she could deliver:
 The Lorelei!

She used to love in a strange kind of fashion,
 With lots of hey, ho-de-ho, hi-de-hi!
And I can guarantee I'm full of passion
 Like the Lorelei.

 I'm treacherous—ja, ja!
Oh, I just can't hold myself in check.
 I'm lecherous—ja, ja!
I want to bite my initials on a sailor's neck.

Each affair had a kick and a wallop,
   For what they craved she could always supply.
I want to be just like that other trollop—
   The Lorelei.

---

*Pardon My English* was a headache from start to finish. The Great Depression was at its deepest when we were asked to do the score for the show. Along with business, employment, and the stock market, the theater too was in terrible shape; and I felt we were lucky to be making a living from *Of Thee I Sing*. In addition, I disliked enormously the central notion of the project—duo-personality or schizophrenia or whatever the protagonist's aberration was supposed to be; so why toil and moil for six months on something we didn't want or need? However, loyalty to producer Aarons, who was broke and who told us if we didn't do the score his potential backers would back out, induced us to go ahead.

During the weeks we were on the road (Philadelphia, Boston, and even a week in Brooklyn), at least five or six librettists and play doctors were called in to work on the book. Herbert Fields was the only one brave enough to allow himself to be billed as librettist. Jack Buchanan, imported to play the duo-personality role (gentleman and gentleman-thief), was so unhappy in it that after a couple of weeks he insisted on buying himself out of the contract. (I heard it cost him twenty thousand dollars, but this is probably an exaggeration.) Whatever business we did, including one good week in Boston, was primarily due to our leading comic, Jack Pearl, whose Baron Munchhausen ("Vas you dere, Sharlie?") on the air attracted some of his radio audience to the theater. Opening night in New York, I stood among the few standees, but only for the first twenty minutes. A bad cold and a lukewarm audience had me home by nine thirty.

\*    \*    \*

I've never known of any theatrical failure where, sooner or later, an author or the stage-manager or one of the backers or some member of the cast didn't reminisce to the effect that there were some pretty good things in it. So, I must add: there were a couple of pretty good songs, like "Isn't It a Pity?" and "My Cousin in Milwaukee," and a couple of pretty good comedy scenes in *Pardon My English, olav hasholom.*

# TRIBUTES TO LIZA ELLIOTT

*(Excerpts from the Glamour Sequence)*

LADY IN THE DARK (1941). Music, Kurt Weill. On a Park Avenue sidewalk, before Liza Elliott's apartment house. Her admirers, *en masse* in faultless evening clothes, sing (*"Allegro giocoso"*):

> We come to serenade the lovely lady we adore.
> She occupies the seventeenth to twenty-second floor.
>> Our lady so seraphic
>> May not be very near us,
>> And with the sound of traffic
>> She may not even hear us—
> But love is wrong without a song,
> So, now as heretofore,
> We come to serenade the lovely lady we adore.

### OH, FABULOUS ONE

> Oh, Fabulous One in your Ivory Tower—
>> Your radiance I fain would see!
> What Mélisande was to Pelléas
>> Are you to me. . . .
> Oh, Fabulous One in your Ivory Tower—
>> My heart and I, they both agree:
> What Juliet was to Romeo
>> Are you to me. . . .
> What Beatrice was to Dante . . .
> What Guinevere was to Lancelot . . .
> What Brünnehilde was to Siegfried . . .
> What Pocahontas was to Captain Smith . . .
> What Martha was to Washington . . .
> What Butterfly was to Pinkerton . . .
> What Calamity Jane was to Buffalo Bill . . .
>> Are you to me. . . .
> Oh, Fabulous One in your Ivory Tower—
>> Oh, Sweet! This is no potpourri!
> What Mélisande was to Pelléas
>> Are you to me!

\*     \*     \*

Liza's maid, in Miss Elliott's boudoir, reads telegrams and letters to her mistress (*"Moderato assai"*):

### HUXLEY

Huxley wants to dedicate his book to you—
  And Stravinsky, his latest sonata.
Seven thousand students say they look to you
  To be at the Yale-Harvard Regatta.
Epstein says you simply have to pose for him.
  Here's the key to the Island of Tobago.
Du Pont wants you wearing the new hose for him.
  Can you christen a battleship in San Diego?

\*     \*     \*

Later, Liza visits the Seventh Heaven Night Club, where all the men rise to acclaim her (*"Allegro giocoso"*):

### GIRL OF THE MOMENT

Oh, girl of the moment
With the smile of the day,
And the charm of the week,
And the grace of the month,
And the looks of the year—
Oh, girl of the moment,
You're my moment ev'ry moment of the time.

Oh, girl of the moment
With the light in your eyes,
And the sun in your hair,
And the rose in your cheeks,
And the laugh in your voice—
Oh, girl of the moment,
In a moment you could make my life sublime.

328

## A Miscellany of Acclaim

In all my flights of fancy
   Your image I drew—
I look at you and can see
   That fancy come true.
Oh, girl of the moment
With the smile of the day,
And the charm of the week,
And the grace of the month,
And the looks of the year—
Oh, girl of the moment,
You're My Moment All the Time!

# THE ILLEGITIMATE DAUGHTER

OF THEE I SING (1931). Music, George Gershwin. Excerpt from Finaletto at the White House, Act II. *"Allegretto giocoso."* Florenz Ames as the French Ambassador.

### Ambassador *(recitative)*

I am the Ambassador of France, and I have come to see a grievous wrong righted. My country is deeply hurt. Not since the days of Louis the Seventh, the Eighth, the Ninth, the Tenth, and possibly the Eleventh, has such a thing happened. You have done a great injustice to a French descendant . . . a lovely girl whose rights have been trampled in the dust!

### Ensemble

Who is she? What's her name?

### Ambassador

Her name is Diana Devereaux.

### Ensemble

Diana Devereaux! Diana Devereaux!
Since when is she of French descent?

### Ambassador

I've been looking up her family tree
And I have found a most important pedigree!

330

## A Miscellany of Acclaim

### THE ILLEGITIMATE DAUGHTER

She's the illegitimate daughter
Of an illegitimate son
Of an illegitimate nephew
　Of Napoleon.
She offers aristocracy
To this bizarre democracy,
Where naught is sacred but the old simoleon!
　I must know why
　You crucify
　My native country
　With this effront'ry—
To the illegitimate daughter
Of an illegitimate son
Of an illegitimate nephew
　Of Napoleon!

*(Ensemble turns on Wintergreen)*

　You so-and-so!
　We didn't know
　She had a tie-up
　So very high up!
She's the illegitimate daughter
Of an illegitimate son
Of an illegitimate nephew
　Of Napoleon!

---

*Genesis of the Illegitimacy.* When we went to California for the film *Delicious* we had already had several discussions with Kaufman and Ryskind on *Of Thee I Sing,* which they were developing. Just before we made the trip they were able to give us a fourteen-page outline of the libretto. In Hollywood between hours on the film we found time to do some work on the operetta

331

and returned to New York with at least two notions in good shape. One was the anthemy campaign title song (later we changed it somewhat); the other was "The Illegitimate Daughter," as is.

Excerpt from page 11 of the scenario: "Throttlebottom also brings out the fact that there is a new angle to the Joan Devereaux matter. [Kaufman and Ryskind later gave Joan a new given name: Diana.] It turns out that she had a French father, so the French government is up in arms about the slight that has been inflicted on her."

"Joan" had to be born in the United States, otherwise couldn't have entered the contest for Mrs. First Lady. Obviously, though, it was far more important to musicalize a French father for her. Should he be a baker in Lyons, or the prefect of police in Dijon, or what? More and more I kept thinking that his political or economic or social importance had to be important, else why France's fuss? Not wishing to use the names of any contemporary personages, I went historical. And, illegitimacy being not too socially disadvantageous among many broad-minded Europeans, I scribbled this possible genealogy for her on the margin of page 11: "She was an illegitimate daughter of an ill. nephew of Louie-Philippe (or Napoleon) so you can't inflict this indignity."

# ALESSANDRO THE WISE

THE FIREBRAND OF FLORENCE (1945). Music, Kurt Weill.
Act I, scene iii. Cellini's studio. Entrance of the Duke of Florence,
who wastes no time in listing his virtues. Melville Cooper and
Soldiers.

*Soldiers*

Make way for the noblest of nobility;
    Make way, or suffer his rebuke.
Bow low, to show humility.
Bow, you peasants, in the presence of the Duke.
    Sing his praises to the skies;
    Hail the man you subsidize—
    Alessandro the Wise!

*Duke*

A hundred years ago or so, the Medici—
    That's my family—began to win renown,
When lovely Florence—be it to her credit!—she
    Got Grandpa*pa's* Pa*pa* to rule the town.

*Soldiers*

Sing out, sing out, or have it played orchestrally—
    Sing out the while you worship at his shrine!

*Duke*

There never was a fellow who, ancestrally,
    Could boast a genealogy like mine:
Lorenzo the Magnificent, and What's-His-Name?–
        The Wondrous;
Plus Other Great who lie in state, and whose acclaim
        Was thund'rous.
Though all were blossoms on the fam'ly tree,
The flower in full bloom you see in me.

333

*Refrain*

I'm aesthetic, poetic;
To beauty I'm sympathetic.

*Soldiers*

A patron of the arts is Alessandro.

*Duke*

My weakness is chicness—
If the lady has no antiqueness.

*Soldiers*

The ladies lose their hearts to Alessandro.

*Duke*

My art collection features Botticelli and Da Vinci;
But also I collect young women who are plump and pinchy.
I sponsor the celestial,
But I don't run down the bestial—
A combination makes 'em idolize

*All*

Alessandro the Wise!

*Second Refrain*

I've a yearning for learning—
To which I am always returning.

*Soldiers*

He's learned a great amount, has Alessandro.

*Duke*

Patrician musician,
And a bit of a mathematician.

*Soldiers*

It figures that figures count—with Alessandro.

334

## A Miscellany of Acclaim

*Duke*

I educate the female mind, the which I do in private.
No matter what erotica their shelves are lacking—I've it.
    With doctrines that embellish
    Both the heavenly and the hellish,
    I make the population idolize

*All*

Alessandro the Wise!

---

*The Firebrand of Florence* had what critics sometimes call an "integrated score." When a review of a musical contains this phrase, the critic usually means that each song in the score helps to forward the story line, or at least fits some characterization or background. But Ned Wayburn, director of my first show, *Two Little Girls in Blue,* had his own notion of an ideal musical setup.

At an early conference with the composers, Vincent Youmans and Paul Lannin, and myself, Wayburn handed us slips of paper indicating what he thought the tentative musical spots in the script called for. I wish I had kept the memo. All I can recall is that there were eighteen or twenty items, with no mention of possible subject matter or type of melody or mood. What we were given was along these lines:

        Act I
    1. Opening
    2. 2/4
    3. 4/4
    4. 6/8
    5. Finaletto
    6. "Oh, Me, Oh, My, Oh, You" [one
           of two songs already written and
           spotted]
    7. 3/4
    8. Finale

And similar fractions for Acts II and III. Obviously, to Wayburn neither the play nor the numbers played were the thing—with his dancing-school proprietorship, tempo alone mattered.

# WINTERGREEN FOR PRESIDENT

OF THEE I SING (1931). Music, George Gershwin. *"Tempo di Marcia."* Opening. A city street across which marches a procession of torchlight campaigners.

> Wintergreen for President!
> Wintergreen for President!
> He's the man the people choose;
> Loves the Irish and the Jews.

---

For some years Strickland Gillilan's "On the Antiquity of Microbes":

> Adam
> Had 'em.

was considered the shortest poem extant. But this record fell when someone (Anon.) came up with "Lines on the Questionable Importance of the Individual":

> I . . .
> Why?

Compared with both of these, the words of "Wintergreen for President" almost equal the length of an Icelandic saga. I imagine, though, that in Songdom "Wintergreen" is one of the shortest lyrics ever.

Additional lines would have been supererogatory. During the four or five minutes of this torchlight-parade number, both title and couplet were repeated several times; but other than the first announcement, neither words nor music were heard—they were drowned out by gales of laughter from the audience when the marchers began showing their campaign banners. There were about twenty of these slogans (all by Kaufman and Ryskind), such as "Win with Wintergreen," "A Vote for Wintergreen Is a

336

Vote for Wintergreen," "The Full Dinner Jacket," "Turn the Reformers Out," "Wintergreen—the Flavor Lasts," and a dozen others.

I once asked George Kaufman what the P. in John P. Wintergreen stood for. His answer: "Why, Peppermint, of course!" with a look that could mean only that any child knew *that*.

\*     \*     \*

It was Oscar Hammerstein, I believe, who in an interview cited "Wintergreen" as an excellent example of words wedded to music. His point was that when one hears the title its music comes immediately to mind, and vice versa.

# Euphoria Revisited

*"I Got Rhythm"*

*"Things Are Looking Up"*

*"There's Nothing Like Marriage for People"*

*"Of Thee I Sing (Baby)"*

*"Who's Complaining?"*

*"I Got Plenty o' Nuthin' "*

# I GOT RHYTHM

GIRL CRAZY (1930). Music, George Gershwin. "Lively, with abandon." Sung by Frisco Kate (Ethel Merman) in isolated Custerville (Ariz.)'s only hot spot—the bar in the town's one hotel.

Days can be sunny,
    With never a sigh;
Don't need what money
    Can buy.

Birds in the tree sing
    Their dayful of song.
Why shouldn't we sing
    Along?

I'm chipper all the day,
    Happy with my lot.
How do I get that way?
    Look at what I've got:

*Refrain*

I got rhythm,
I got music,
I got my man—
Who could ask for anything more?

I got daisies
In green pastures,
I got my man—
Who could ask for anything more?

341

Old Man Trouble,
I don't mind him—
You won't find him
'Round my door.

I got starlight,
I got sweet dreams,
I got my man—
Who could ask for anything more—
Who could ask for anything more?

---

*Rhythm and Little Rhyme.* Filling in the seventy-three syllables of the refrain wasn't as simple as it sounds. For over two weeks I kept fooling around with various titles and with sets of double rhymes for the trios of short two-foot lines. I'll ad lib a dummy to show what I was at: "Roly-Poly, / Eating solely / Ravioli, / Better watch your diet or bust. / / Lunch or dinner, / You're a sinner. / Please get thinner. / Losing all that fat is a must." Yet, no matter what series of double rhymes—even pretty good ones—I tried, the results were not quite satisfactory; they seemed at best to give a pleasant and jingly Mother Goose quality to a tune which should throw its weight around more. Getting nowhere, I then found myself not bothering with the rhyme scheme I'd considered necessary (aaab, cccb) and experimenting with non-rhyming lines like (dummy): "Just go forward; / Don't look backward; / And you'll soon be / Winding up ahead of the game." This approach felt stronger, and finally I arrived at the present refrain (the rhymed verse came later), with only "more—door" and "mind him—find him" the rhymes. Though there is nothing remarkable about all this, it was a bit daring for me who usually depended on rhyme insurance.

But what *is* singular about this lyric is that the phrase "Who could ask for anything more?" occurs four times—which, ordinarily and unquestionably, should make that phrase the title. Somehow the first line of the refrain sounded more arresting and provocative.

Therefore, "I Got Rhythm." (Incidentally, although rejected for this song, "Who Could Ask for Anything More?" later did make it as a title—twice, in fact—when Kay Swift and Ethel Merman each at different times used it for their autobiographies.)

*Got.* In some entertainment reviews and on some disc labels this song is called "I've Got Rhythm." I appreciate the correctors' efforts to formalize the title, but I'm sticking with the more direct "I Got Rhythm" for this tune. Although "got" for some centuries has been accepted as a strengthener in "I've got" and "I have got" —and although "got" as the past of "get" generally means "acquired" or "achieved"—neither of these uses obtains here. In the title and refrain of this song (also in "I Got Plenty o' Nuthin' ") "got" is heard in its most colloquial form—the one used for the present tense instead of "have," and the one going back to my childhood: e.g., "I got a toothache" didn't mean "I had a toothache," but only "I have" one. Thumbing through many authorities on usage, style, and dialect, I find no discussion of "got" as a complete substitute for "have." This is somewhat surprising when one considers, say, how often and for how many years the spiritual "All o' God's Chillun Got Shoes" ("I got shoes, you got shoes") has been heard.

P.S. Obviously, I've got nothing against "I've got" since the verse ends with "Look at what I've got." The reason in this instance is that the musically less assertive and regularly rhymed verse seems to require the more conventional phrasing.

# THINGS ARE LOOKING UP

A DAMSEL IN DISTRESS (1937). Music, George Gershwin. *"Moderato e cantabile."* Sung by Fred Astaire to Joan Fontaine on the downs of Totleigh Castle, located in Upper Pelham-Grenville, Wodehouse, England.

If I should suddenly start to sing
Or stand on my head—or anything,
Don't think that I've lost my senses;
It's just that my happiness finally commences.
The long, long ages of dull despair
Are turning into thin air,
And it seems that suddenly I've
Become the happiest man alive.

*Refrain*

Things are looking up!
I've been looking the landscape over
And it's covered with four leaf clover.
Oh, things are looking up
Since love looked up at me.

Bitter was my cup—
But no more will I be the mourner,
For I've certainly turned the corner.
Oh, things are looking up
Since love looked up at me.

See the sunbeams—
Ev'ry one beams
Just because of you.
Love's in session,
And my depression
Is unmistakably through.

## Euphoria Revisited

Things are looking up!
It's a great little world we live in!
Oh, I'm happy as a pup
Since love looked up
At me.

---

*Parental Note.* Although this song never reached anywhere near as many ears as, say, "A Foggy Day" from the same film, it is based on a good title and a graceful tune; and I like it. For that matter, I like the majority of the songs I have been connected with. And I can't conceive of any songwriter not feeling the same way about his output. The marriage of words and music gives birth over the years to a catalogful of progeny. Many of the offspring turn out to be lame and halting, or too frenetic, or over-sophisticated, or something. But the parents manage generally to find some excuse for, even some endearing quality in, these disappointers: *This* one was ahead of its time; *that* one stammered a bit—true—but did sing like an angel; *yonder* got into bad hands, &c. Metaphorical excursion over, over to the over-all point:

Next to the antecedence of words or music, the question most frequently asked is: "What's your own favorite song?" And the favorite answer of some writers is: "The latest one." But generally, and more truthful, is: "Most of them."

\*    \*    \*

*Losing the Rhyme.* The reader or reciter of rhymed poetry is of course more concerned with meaning than with rhyme, so naturally doesn't pause at the end of a run-on line to emphasize the rhyming. In entertainment song, though, I feel that rhyme, even in a run-on couplet, ought to be observed—or at least not negated—especially when the music calls for pause or breath. An example of

345

this perhaps not too important point shows up in a recent recording of "Things Are Looking Up." The vocalist sings the vest thus:

> And it seems that suddenly—
> I've become the happiest man alive.

Personally I'd rather hear:

> And it seems that suddenly I've—
> Become the happiest man alive.

# THERE'S NOTHING LIKE MARRIAGE
# FOR PEOPLE

PARK AVENUE (1946). Music, Arthur Schwartz. "Ecstatically."
Finale, Act I. Sung at Mrs. Ogden Bennett's house, Long Island,
by an octette of the much-married-and-divorced set. The husbands
(H) were played by Arthur Margetson, Robert Chisholm,
Charles Purcell, Raymond Walburn; the wives (W) by Leonora
Corbett, Marthe Errolle, Ruth Matteson, Mary Wickes. Husbands
and wives, having just announced the newest matrimonial permuta-
tion possible among themselves, enthusiastically endorse (for the
third or fourth time in their years) Marriage and True-Happiness-
At-Last.

1

*W:*   Imagine living with someone
        Who's longing to live with you!

*H:*   Imagine signing a lease together;
        And hanging a Matisse together!

*W:*   Oh, what felicity / In domesticity!

*H:*   Let no one disparage / Marriage!

*W:*   Being alone and breaking bread together—
        Reading *The New Yorker* in bed together—

*H:*   Starting a family tree together—
        Voting for the G.O.P. together—

*Refrain*

*All:*   There's nothing like marriage for people—
        It means you're living at last.

347

W:        Carry me over the threshold!

H:        When you her flesh hold,
          On life you get a fresh hold.

*All:*  How can we miss? There'll be bliss unsurpassed.

W:        Give me That Kingdom
          Of Wedding Ringdom!

*All:*  Let there be ding-a-dong up in the steeple,
              And thousands of old shoes to throw;
          Nothing's as wonderful as marriage for people—
              And we are the people who know!

2

W:  Imagine signing a license
      And finally settling down.

H:  Vowing always to be true together—
      Paddling your own canoe together—

W:  No more philandering / When on my hand a ring.

H:  Existence is lifeless / Wifeless.

W:  Shopping at Cartier's together—
      Giving dinner partiers together—

H:  Palm Beach in the late fall together—
      Getting coats of tan in the altogether—

                    *Refrain*

*All:*  There's nothing like marriage for people—
              It means you're living at last.

W:        Hurry, let's call up the minister!

H:          Why be a sinister
            Old bachelor or spinister?

*All:*  Give me the feast, not the fast of the past.

H:          If there's misogyny,
            You can't have progeny.

*All:*  Let there be ding-a-dong up in the steeple,
            And heaven on earth here below;
            Nothing's as wonderful as marriage for people—
            AND WE ARE THE PEOPLE WHO KNOW!

---

If it is noticed that the seventh and eighth lines in the first verse do not parallel metrically the equivalent couplet in the second verse, that's because the verse music was more or less *Recitativo*. This can allow for freedom in the number of syllables. For instance, the following couplet:

Finishing a magnum of Lanson together—
Making application at Groton for our gran'son together—

was funny to us because so many syllables were packed into the second line to be sung rapidly in the same time limit as the first line. But its allusions were too special to use.

\*          \*          \*

In *Park Avenue,* George S. Kaufman, Nunnally Johnson, Arthur Schwartz, and I thought we would have a novelty show—a so-called "smart" show—if only for the reason that it pertained to the upper-bracket-income-and-black-tie set as against four or five years of nothing but costume and period operettas on Broadway. Novelty or not, there were two reasons for our flopping: (A) charm wasn't enough to sustain the second act; (B) evidently di-

349

vorce is a ticklish subject to be funny about for an entire show. In Boston during the first week of our tryout, Arthur Schwartz told me that a friend of his, whom he had invited to see the show, cried through most of it. She had recently been divorced and just couldn't take it.

# OF THEE I SING (BABY)

OF THEE I SING (1931). Music, George Gershwin. "Slowly and with much expression." Inside Madison Square Garden. Presidential candidate John P. Wintergreen (his platform: LOVERS! VOTE FOR JOHN AND MARY!) sings The Official Campaign Love Song to Mary Turner, his bride-to-be. Wintergreen, William Gaxton; Mary, Lois Moran.

From the Island of Manhattan to the Coast of Gold,
From North to South, from East to West,
You are the love I love the best.
You're the dream girl of the sweetest story ever told;
A dream I've sought both night and day
For years through all the U.S.A.
The star I've hitched my wagon to
Is very obviously you.

*Refrain*

Of thee I sing, baby—
Summer, autumn, winter, spring, baby.
You're my silver lining,
You're my sky of blue;
There's a lovelight shining
Just because of you.

Of thee I sing, baby—
You have got that certain thing, baby!
Shining star and inspiration,
Worthy of a mighty nation—
Of thee I sing!

---

When we first played this sentimental political campaign song for those connected with the show, there were one or two strong

351

objectors who thought that juxtaposing the dignified "of thee I sing" with a slangy "baby" was going a bit too far. Our response (a frequent one over the years) was that, naturally, we'd replace it with something else if the paying audience didn't take to it. This was one time we were pretty sure that they would; and they did. Opening night, and even weeks later, one could hear a continuous "Of thee I sing, *Baby!*" when friends and acquaintances greeted one another in the lobby at intermission time.

\*       \*       \*

*Euterpe and the Lucky Lyric-writer.* The authorities on respectable English and formal prose warn against sliding into slang or into polysyllabic humor or the mixed metaphor or the genteelism or the inadvertent jingle or overuse of the foreign phrase, and other verbal mire. And, especially, sentences must never get bogged down in, or become contaminated by, the cliché. Inasmuch as I have little to do with formal prose, I bow respectfully to all the advice, rules, and definitions given by the usage and abusage arbiters—going along with them all the way from Ambiguity to Zeugma. But, alas, much of what they advocate doesn't apply to the lyric-writer. The jingle quality (inadvertent or deliberate), for instance, is part and parcel (oops! cliché) of lyric-writing. As for *cliché* itself:

Eric Partridge, in his *A Dictionary of Clichés,* lists alphabetically —leaving out X and Z—over two thousand phrases that "careful speakers and scrupulous writers shrink from. . . ." Under *A* are such examples as: "as a matter of fact" and "accidents will happen"; under *Y:* "your guess is as good as mine" and "young in heart." In a matter of minutes I have selected an example from each section: "at (a person's) beck and call"; "build upon sand"; "cross the Rubicon"; "dance attendance on"; "eat humble pie"; "flash in the pan"; "good Queen Bess"; "hitch one's wagon to a star"; "I mean to say"; "je ne sais quoi"; "keep one's nose to the grindstone"; "lay one's cards on the table"; "make the welkin ring"; "non compos mentis"; "on one's mettle"; "pay the piper (and call the tune)"; (nothing in *Q*); "red-letter day"; "six of one and half a dozen of the other"; "this vale of tears"; "upset the apple cart";

"vanish into thin air"; "(the) writing on the wall"; "year in (and) year out."

Why this deluge of watered-down phrase? If not immediately obvious, the answer is: because I have used every one of them, and hundreds of others, in songs. So, I list them not flauntingly, nor to thumb-nose, but because the literary cliché is an integral part of lyric-writing. If I were doing editorials I might never write, say: "Things have came to a pretty pass" (re some disturbing condition), but I like it when it is sung to start the verse of "Let's Call the Whole Thing Off." The phrase that is trite and worn-out when appearing in print usually becomes, when heard fitted to an appropriate musical turn, revitalized, and seems somehow to revert to its original provocativeness.

As Congreve didn't quite put it:

Not only hath music charms to soothe the savage breast,
To soften rocks, undo the clenchéd fist . . .
It refurbisheth the puissance the cliché once possessed.
(How fortunate the priv'leged lyricist!)

# WHO'S COMPLAINING?

COVER GIRL (1944). Music, Jerome Kern. Sung by Phil Silvers as "Genius," Master of Ceremonies in McGuire's Brooklyn Night Club. Time: Period of comparative civilian austerity during World War II.

### 1

My butcher shop, my grocery
Can keep on saying, "No sir-ee!"
    But lack of this or that
    Doesn't knock me flat;
    For in times like these,
    Life's no life of ease.

### Burthen

Who's complaining?
I'm not complaining;
You'll see we'll see the thing through.
Because of Axis trickery
My coffee now is chicory,
    And I can rarely purloin
    A sirloin.

But—no complaining
Through the campaigning;
Who cares if carrots are few?
I'll feed myself on artichokes
Until that Nazi party chokes—
    So long as they don't ration
    My passion
    For you.

*Euphoria Revisited*

### 2

Who's complaining?
I'm not complaining;
That's one thing we mustn't do.
I go to work by bicycle,
My house is like an icicle,
　　And oh, my lack of butter
　　Is utter.

But—no complaining
Through the campaigning;
Don't ask what's in the ragout.
All rationing by OPA
Is heaven and U-toe-pee-a—
　　So long as they don't ration
　　My passion
　　For you.

### The Girls

Who's complaining?
I'm not complaining,
When taking on is taboo.
My vanity may wonder where
To get new clothes and underwear;
　　My legs may be forgotten
　　In cotton.

But—no complaining
Through the campaigning;
I'll raise no hullabaloo.
My nails may lose their brilliancy,
But who cares what civilians see—
　　So long as they don't ration
　　My passion
　　For you.

355

*Updating.* Lyrics like this one, written in, and for, a special period and using topical allusions, inevitably become dated in a matter of years. For instance, few of the younger generation today would know that OPA stands for Office of Price Administration, a vital government agency during World War II. Sometimes an allusive-of-the-period lyric can be updated in later years, but this is a dangerous proceeding if the original is well known. A New York production of *The Mikado* once updated many of the references in "They'll None of 'Em Be Missed," a revision roundly denounced by the drama critics.

In the revival of *Of Thee I Sing,* twenty years after the original production, I agreed that, along with some revisions in the book, some somewhat dated and obscure references in the lyrics and recitatives should be revised. Naturally I tried for changes that weren't too noticeably updated. One example: In 1932, when President Wintergreen tried to sluff off comment on the girl he had jilted, the White House reporters insisted:

> We don't want to know about the moratorium,
>> Or how near we are to beer,
>>> Or about the League of Nations,
>>> Or the seventeen vacations
>> You have had since you've been here.

By 1952 the Hoover Moratorium was only for historians, Prohibition had been ousted for almost a generation, the League of Nations had given way to the United Nations. Resting up, though, was still in vogue; so, now the reporters sang:

> We don't want to know about your foreign policy,
>> Or the latest party smear,
>>> Or the budget innovations,
>>> Or the seventeen vacations
>> You have had since you've been here.

In one instance, however, against my better judgment—because it was a fairly well-known song—I revised the Depression couplet in "Who Cares?":

> Who cares what banks fail in Yonkers,
> Long as you've got a kiss that conquers?

to one I considered pretty good:

> Who cares how history rates me,
> Long as your kiss intoxicates me?

Which change, of course, went by unnoticed by the new audiences. But several show-song *aficionados* (those with watchman's vigilance over any songs they favor—whether well known or obscure) looked askance at me as though I were trespassing upon their proprietary rights.

# I GOT PLENTY O' NUTHIN'

PORGY AND BESS (1935). Music, George Gershwin. *"Moderato con gioja*—Banjo Song." Lyric in collaboration with DuBose Heyward. Act II, scene i: Todd Duncan as "Porgy—at window—happily."

Oh, I got plenty o' nuthin',
An' nuthin's plenty fo' me.
I got no car, got no mule, I got no misery.
De folks wid plenty o' plenty
Got a lock on dey door,
'Fraid somebody's a-goin' to rob 'em
While dey's out a-makin' more.
What for?
I got no lock on de door,
(Dat's no way to be).
Dey can steal de rug from de floor,
Dat's O.K. wid me,
'Cause de things dat I prize,
Like de stars in de skies,
All are free.
Oh, I got plenty o' nuthin',
An' nuthin's plenty fo' me.
I got my gal, got my song,
Got Hebben de whole day long.
(No use complainin'!)
Got my gal, got my Lawd, got my song.

*Euphoria Revisited*

I got plenty o' nuthin',
An' nuthin's plenty fo' me.
I got de sun, got de moon, got de deep blue sea.
De folks wid plenty o' plenty,
Got to pray all de day.
Seems wid plenty you sure got to worry
How to keep de Debble away,
A-way.
I ain't a-frettin' 'bout Hell
Till de time arrive.
Never worry long as I'm well,
Never one to strive
To be good, to be bad—
What the hell! I is glad
I's alive.
Oh, I got plenty o' nuthin'
An' nuthin's plenty fo' me.
I got my gal, got my song,
Got Hebben de whole day long.
(No use complainin'!)
Got my gal, got my Lawd, got my song!

---

From a letter to Frank Durham, published in his *DuBose Heyward* (University of South Carolina Press, 1954):

"DuBose and I were in George's workroom. George felt there was a spot where Porgy might sing something lighter and gayer than the melodies and recitatives he had been given in Act I. He went to the piano and began to improvise. A few preliminary chords and in less than a minute a well-rounded, cheerful melody. 'Something like that,' he said. Both DuBose and I had the same reaction: 'That's it! Don't look any further.' 'You really think so?' and, luckily, he recaptured it and played it again. A title popped into my mind. (This was one out of only three or four times in my career that a possible title hit me on first hearing a tune. Usually I sweat for days.) ' "I got plenty o' nuthin'," ' I said tentatively.

[And a moment later the obvious balance line, 'An' nuthin's plenty for me.'] Both George and DuBose seemed delighted with it, so with this assurance I said, 'Fine. I'll get to work on it later.' DuBose: 'Ira, would you mind if I tried my hand at it? So far everything I've done has been set by George and I've never written words to music. If it's all right with you I'd love to take the tune along with me to Charleston.' I think we discussed generally the mood and even arrived at a couple of lines. Two weeks later DuBose sent me a version that had many useable lines; many, however, looked good on paper but were awkward when sung. This is no reflection on DuBose's ability. It takes years and years of experience to know that such a note cannot take such a syllable, that many a poetic line can be unsingable, that many an ordinary line fitted into the proper musical phrase can sound like a million. So on this song I did have to do a bit of 'polishing.' All in all, I'd consider this a 50–50 collaborative effort."

✳     ✳     ✳

This, as the letter tells, is the only instance wherein DuBose tried working to a tune. All his fine and poetic lyrics were set to music by George with scarcely a syllable being changed—an aspect of this composer's versatility not generally recognized. These many years . . . and I can still shake my head in wonder at the reservoir of musical inventiveness, resourcefulness, and craftsmanship George could dip into. And no fraternal entrancement, my wonderment. He takes two simple quatrains of DuBose's, studies the lines, and in a little while a lullaby called "Summertime" emerges —delicate and wistful, yet destined to be sung over and over again. Out of the libretto's dialogue he takes Bess's straight, unrhymed speech which starts: "What you want wid Bess? She's gettin' old now," and it becomes a rhythmic aria; then he superimposes Crown's lines, "What I wants wid other woman? I gots a woman," and now is heard at once a moving and exultant duet. Not a syllable of DuBose's poignant "My Man's Gone Now" is changed as the composer sets it to waltz time, adds the widow's heart-rending wail between stanzas, and climaxes the tragic la-

360

ment with an ascending glissando—resulting in one of the most memorable moments in the American musical theater.

If I have stumbled into the field of the musicologist without being a musician, all I'm trying to say is that George could be as original and distinctive when musicalizing words (as in the above examples, plus "A Woman Is a Sometime Thing," "The Buzzard Song," and others) as when composing music which later would require words ("It Ain't Necessarily So," "There's a Boat Dat's Leavin' Soon for New York," "Bess, You Is My Woman Now," and others). Regardless of which procedure was used, the resultant compositions sang so naturally that I doubt if any listener, lacking the mentions in this note, could tell which came first—the words or the music.

# AFTERWORD

Anyone may turn up with a hit song, as evidenced by any number of one-hit writers. What, however, I hope some of the notes have succeeded in indicating—if only between the lines—is that a career of lyric-writing isn't one that anyone can easily muscle in on; that if the lyricist who lasts isn't a W. S. Gilbert he is at least literate and conscientious; that even when his words at times sound like something off the cuff, lots of hard work and experience have made them so. And I do believe that generally I am speaking not only for myself but for—in any order you like—Porter, Fields, Berlin, Mercer, Lerner, Loesser, Dietz, Wodehouse, Comden and Green, Hammerstein, Hart, Harburg, and two or three others whose work I respect.

It may seem strange to end a book with a definition—and a borrowed one at that. And doubtless the two gentlemen who wrote the scholarly article on SONG for the *Britannica* didn't have popular and musical-comedy song in mind. But I can think of no better way to conclude what much of this book has been about than to quote their opening statement:

> SONG is the joint art of words and music, two arts under emotional pressure coalescing into a third. The relation and balance of the two arts is a problem that has to be resolved anew in every song that is composed.

# Index of Song Titles

(* indicates first appearance in print)

i

# Index of Song Titles

# General Index

# General Index

iv

# General Index

# General Index

# General Index

# General Index